Revolutionary Versus Loyalist

Primary Sources in
American History

CONSULTING EDITOR
Grady McWhiney, University of British Columbia

Revolutionary Versus Loyalist

The First American

Civil War

1774–1784

EDITED BY LESLIE F. S. UPTON

University of British Columbia

BLAISDELL PUBLISHING COMPANY

A Division of Ginn and Company

WALTHAM, MASSACHUSETTS / TORONTO / LONDON

Foreword

Thorough understanding of the events and trends that make up our history cannot be acquired merely by reading textbook interpretations. It is essential also to study the basis of such interpretations. *The Primary Sources in American History Series* provides the student with materials in the form of letters, diaries, memoirs, pamphlets, and newspaper accounts written during or shortly after major historical events — documents up to now buried in the library and often unavailable.

Edited and introduced by a leading scholar, each volume either concentrates on discussion of a given topic in contemporary letters, newspaper articles, and essays or presents new editions of classic eyewitness accounts of significant events. Though generations removed from an actual occurrence, the student has the opportunity to understand it in depth and to apply his analytical and critical powers to it. He then also can compare his own interpretations with those provided by general histories, biographies, and monographs.

GRADY MCWHINEY

Contents

Introduction

This collection of readings presents the American Revolution as a civil war. The simple fact that the Declaration of Independence was attended by civil war is often forgotten, and the events of the Revolution are thereby robbed of much of their drama. Without the dimension of loyalism, the Revolution becomes a safe consensus movement, predictable in its origins, predictable in its outcome. The Revolution may have been completed in the minds of Americans by 1775, as John Adams later claimed, but it is necessary to distinguish between a revolution in the mind and a revolution under arms. There is little doubt that by 1775 all Americans were agreed in demanding internal self-government, and they had molded recent events and interpreted the more distant past to justify this claim. But revolution is still a decisive step: a man may think his government corrupt, but he does not, for that reason, go out and shoot a policeman.

Americans, in writing the history of these times, have presented the revolutionary as the norm, the peaceable citizen as the aberration. The Revolution quickly became an establishment from which dissent could not be tolerated, and this attitude has continued down to the present day. For generations, the most pervasive theme followed by American historians has been the development of the covenant brought to the New World by the Pigrim Fathers. These were men of sufficient moral stature to make an agreement with God, who would take them as His chosen people if they would establish His city in the wilderness. The purity of this new foundation would rest largely on the repudiation of the accumulated evils of Europe which had defiled the elect. The American Revolution, which brought a political break from Europe, was, from this point of view, preordained, a necessary cleansing, a fulfillment of the covenant. But this spirit of American distinctiveness and sense of mission did not disappear after the Revolution. Over the years, these traits were both modified and expanded, secularised into the "American Dream" and the "American Way of Life." The spirit of the covenant lived on, complete with its pride, its self-assurance, and feeling of superiority to the European past.

Yet the incredible thing was that many Americans chose to step outside this covenant at the time of the Revolution by refusing to repudiate Britain and all her works. This fact has been regarded as both extraordinary and embarrassing: extraordinary because so many failed to appreciate the privilege of being American; embarrassing because it questioned the validity of the whole covenant idea of a chosen people. If Americans in large numbers, in the hundreds of thousands, were unconvinced, it was just possible that the whole American experiment was a failure, perhaps a fraud, and existence in the New World devoid of meaning.

For raising this doubt, the loyalists have been severly punished by historians: they have been ignored, relegated to an uncomplimentary paragraph or two. Abandoning the covenant and challenging the "American-ness" of America are high crimes. In addition, the loyalists failed, and few crimes are more heinous to an American than failure. As the loyalists did not "contribute," they have no place in the onward sweep of American history. This is only appropriate for those who tried to give the lie to the idea that the Revolution was part of the Divine plan for Americans, for those who ruined what should

have been a grand epic of brave men standing shoulder to
shoulder against a European despot, by creating instead a
sorry tale of brother fighting brother, with all the moral un-
certainties and shame that civil war produces.

This collection presents the reader with the viewpoint of
both revolutionaries and loyalists, Americans all. A respectable pedigree of revolutionary writing can be established dating
back to 1760, but the loyalist pamphleteer does not come on
the scene until 1774. The reason is not hard to find, for not
until that year did it appear that there might be a revolution in
the making. The tumults that had accompanied the Stamp
Act crisis may indeed have bordered on the revolutionary, but
their very violence had produced a revulsion in all right-think-
ing men. It was unbelievable that the prosperous colonials
would indulge in such a precarious exercise as rebellion. Since
the loyalists defended the political framework they knew, they
could not be expected to spring to its defense before it was
attacked.

The years covered in this book, 1774 to 1784, fall into three
divisions. Through 1774 and 1775 there was doubt whether the
crisis would result in the adoption of an inflexible position by
either side. For a few months there was genuine literary debate
between partisans and critics of Congress. The contestants
fitted each other into the customary nomenclature of colonial
politics as Whig and Tory. Even so, from the first, loyalist
writers whose veil of anonymity was pierced were subjected
to mob harassment and their works were frequently destroyed.

In the course of 1776 the Revolution became official, and
the question then was whether the differences between Britain
and the republic were negotiable. Loyalists could continue to
write from safety within the British lines, but if their works
ever reached rebel territory they were, understandably, destroyed as enemy propaganda. For the loyalist outside British
lines there was no further question of debate; such men were
now dealt with by more practical methods. The revolutionary
attitude to the loyalists can best be judged from the records of

the committees of safety in the various states. Perversity was summarily punished: loyalists were smeared in the press, deprived of their possessions, expelled from their jobs and evicted from their homes. Those pamphleteers who still noticed the loyalists, did not argue any longer but indulged in ungentle satire or outright denunciation. The treason of the loyal fitted well into one of the standard vehicles of communication of the times, the pulpit oration, the Jeremiad that called down Divine wrath on the unbeliever.

By 1782, with American independence assured, the question arose whether the loyalists should be allowed to stay on in their native land or be banished forever. This debate was exclusively for Americans of impeccable revolutionary credentials; loyalists still in the states were perforce in hiding and had no access to the press. The loyalists within British lines had no more to say to their fellow-countrymen and concentrated their energies on gaining compensation from the imperial government.

At each stage of the Revolution great issues had been argued out by Americans speaking from a common background. Revolutionary pamphleteers had had a variety of targets to aim at: the king, his ministry, his troops, his supporters. Loyalist writers denounced one group of foemen: those who would lead their people astray. The clash of ideas proved to be an unequal contest, yet the very zeal of the revolutionaries in stopping the circulation of loyalist ideas was an oblique testimony to the strength of this dissent. It is apparent that loyalist writings failed to reach a large number of Americans. Consequently, these ideas are not important in molding public opinion, but in expressing views that kept hundreds of thousands of Americans out of the revolutionary movement. The point is not whether the loyalists' arguments were accepted; suffice it that they were presented.

The articulate loyalists were conservatives in the best sense of the word. They would accept change, sympathising with radical criticism of the mother country, but they maintained an unshakable faith in the merit and adaptability of existing institutions. They would stop short of destroying the political framework of the society they knew. The enforced exodus of the loyalists robbed the United States of that most stabilising of political influences, a truly conservative element. The men who made the constitution of 1789 were not conservatives but continentalists building on their revolutionary experience. American conservatism had no point of reference, for the conservative's past, like every other American's, was in revolution. As a result, what has been called conservatism in the United States has too often been an emotional and temporary reaction to the particular events of a particular day, based on no principle. The United States has still to reconstruct a rational conservative sentiment, which, once repudiated, has never returned.

LESLIE F. S. UPTON

PART ONE

CHAPTER 1   Loyalist Meets
Revolutionary

For two years before the Declaration of Independence was signed, loyalists were subjected to mob harassment. Demonstrations stopped short of bloodshed, but the consequences could be unpleasant: being stripped naked and dipped in tar, ridden on rails, or shut in a room and smoked by a fire of green logs. Sewall and Boucher, whose adventures are described below, were both fortunate in escaping bodily harm; yet although these particular episodes had their humorous side, both men learned their lesson and quit home for England. Their property was eventually confiscated, and they were banished under pain of death should they return to America.

The first excerpt describes an attack on the house of Judge Jonathan Sewall at Cambridge, Massachusetts. Fortunately for him, he was not at home at the time. Sewall (1728–1796) was born into one of the most important Boston families, whose ancestors had come over in 1634. A lawyer, he became provincial attorney general in 1767, and in the following year was appointed judge of vice-admiralty. He was a close friend of John Adams, but broke with him at the Revolution. Sewall came to the attention of the patriots as one who had signed a testimonial address to the unpopular Governor Hutchinson. An exile in England, Sewall lived at Bristol until 1788 when he

moved to Halifax, Nova Scotia. He died in the loyalist city of
Saint John, New Brunswick.

Jonathan Boucher (1738–1806) was a clergyman of the
Church of England who became conspicuous when faced with
the problem of following the monarchical sentiments in the
Book of Common Prayer while those around him were in-
creasingly revolutionary in their outlook. Boucher had come
to Virginia in 1759 as a private tutor. Three years later he was
ordained in the Episcopal Church, and in 1770 moved to St.
Ann's Parish in Annapolis, Maryland. A friend of the governor, he came to know the leading men of the area, and in 1772
bought himself a large plantation. He fled to England in September, 1775.

---

*Untitled paper with marginal notation "Tea Notes 1774" in Sewell
Papers.*

Public Archives of Canada, Ottawa.
Reprinted by permission of the Dominion Archivist

On Thursday evening September 1, 1774 there was a riotous
assembling of about 40 or 50 men & boys in the town of Cambridge — I passed by them several times in the course of the
evening carefully observing their number strength & movements — About half past 11 or at 12 o'clock in the night, thinking that they had dispersed in a great measure & perceiving that
they had been in indifferent spirits the whole evening, I went
to Judge Sewall's & informed Mrs Sewall that I believed there
was no danger of a visit from them at that time of night; but
if they came, they were so little used to acts of violence that I
thought we might safely venture to resist them. About ½
hour after being alarmed with the noise of their coming, &
having secured the Windows & Doors as well as we could, we
repaired to Mrs Sewall's Chamber; they came shouting & blow-
ing a horn & Mrs Sewall threw up the window when they had
got to the house & asked them what they would have — they

replied Mr. Sewall, — she told them he was not at home, but
had gone to Boston in the morning & had not returned since;
on which they exclaimed she was a damned liar &c that he was
in the house & they would search the house for him & have
him; — on which there was a tumultous noise, but Mrs Sewall
begged to be heard, & being a little more silent, she observed
to them that being a woman she expected civil treatment from
them as she had & would treat them; they exclaimed that he
was an enemy to his country & have him they would — Mrs
Sewall begged them not to disturb her — that being alone she
hoped they would not treat her or her children ill, & if they
would go away, they should have anything she could give them
out of the house. They swore they would search the house &
immediately burst open the door. Finding they had entered &
hearing them below, Mr. Chipman, Mr. Coffin & myself, together with a servant of Judge Sewall's, being all the males that
were in the house ran downstairs, attacked them & by an active
& vigorous application of the argumentum baculinum drove
them out & Mr. Coffin declared that he would blow the first
man's brains out, that offered to enter again. As soon as those
who had entered were attacked by the besieged, & continually
after, those without played their artillery of stones & brickbats
against the windows. The door being shut, & they being en-
raged by the explosion of a gun in the entry near the front
window tho' without the least design of hurting & at a different side of the house from where we supposed the mob were,
they went into the front yard & broke those windows. We
then went out to them & declared that the gun went off acci-
dentally, that we were sorry for it as it was agreed upon since
we had got them out of the house not to fire but on the last
extremity; yet that we were determined to defend ourselves at
the risque of our lives & they might depend upon resistance at
all events if they offered to reenter. We begged them to consider the distress this might occasion to Mrs Sewall & family &
to disperse. They appeared to be satisfied about the gun at
last, told us we had fought like brave fellows & if we would

give them something to drink they would not go to Judge
Lee's as they intended but would disperse which they did after
drinking a few glasses of wine & cordially bid each other
Good-Night.

NB There did not appear to be many more than 30 at Judge
Sewall's.

JONATHAN BOUCHER

Reminiscences of an American Loyalist, 1738–1789, *Jonathan
Bouchier, ed.*

*Houghton Mifflin Co., Boston and New York, 1925, pp. 112–113,
118–124. Reprinted by permission of Houghton Mifflin Co.*

. . . It was proper however and necessary that at least I
should continue to go to church. My wife's uncle Mr. Addison's parish was supposed to be somewhat quieter than mine;
and as this was the case, and my estate also lay in it, I left
Queen Anne and removed to The Lodge, where I officiated as
Mr. Addison's curate; having put a Mr. Harrison, brother to
the gentleman of that name who was afterwards Mr. Washington's secretary, into the cure of my parish. In the usual
and regular course of preaching I happened one Sunday to
recommend peaceableness; on which a Mr. Lee and sundry
others, supposing my sermon to be what they called a stroke
at the times, rose up and left the church. This was a signal to
the people to consider every sermon of mine as hostile to the
views and interests of America; and accordingly I never after
went into a pulpit without something very disagreeable hap-
pening. I received sundry messages and letters threatening me
with the most fatal consequences if I did not (not desist from
preaching at all, but) preach what should be agreeable to the
friends of America. All the answer I gave to these threats
was in my sermons, in which I uniformly and resolutely declared that I never could suffer any merely human authority to
intimidate me from performing what in my conscience I be-

lieved and knew to be my duty to God and His Church. And for more than six months I preached, when I did preach, with a pair of loaded pistols lying on the cushion; having given notice that if any man, or body of men, could possibly be so lost to all sense of decency and propriety as to attempt really to do what had been long threatened, that is, to drag me out of my own pulpit, I should think myself justified before God and man in repelling violence by violence. . . .

*   *   *

The principles and ways of thinking of Whigs and Tories, or of Republicans and Loyalists, are hardly more different than are their tempers. The latter have a foolish good-nature and improvidence about them which leads them often to hurt their own interests by promoting those of their adversaries, when the objects for which they contended are removed; but the former never forgives, never ceases to effect his purposes of being revenged on those he has once called his enemies. Mr. Sprigg was a thorough Whig, and I perhaps as thorough a Loyalist; as appeared on the last fracas of the kind in which I was involved, and which now soon took place.

A public fast was ordained. In America, as in the Grand Rebellion in England, much execution was done by sermons. Those persons who have read any out of the great number of Puritan sermons that were then printed as well as preached, will cease to wonder that so many people were worked up into such a state of frenzy; and I who either heard, or heard of, many similar discourses from the pulpits in America, felt the effects of them no less than they had before been felt here. My curate was but a weak brother, yet a strong Republican, i.e., as far as he knew how. The sermon he had preached on a former fast, though very silly, was still more exceptionable as contributing to blow the coals of sedition. Its silliness perhaps made it even more mischievous; for to be very popular, it is, I believe, necessary to be very like the bulk of the people, that is, wrong-headed, ignorant, and prone to resist authority. And I am persuaded, whenever it happens that a really sensible man becomes the idol of the people, it must be owing to his possessing a talent of letting himself down to their level. It remains to be proved, however, that ever a really sensible person did take this part; I think the contrary may be proved. As, however, Mr. Harrison's practice as well as preaching were now beginning to be exceptionable, that is, by his setting about and promoting factious Associations and subscriptions, it was thought necessary that on the approaching fast-day, which was a day of great expectation, I should make a point of appearing in my own pulpit; and the Governor waited on me on purpose to press my doing so.

On my informing Mr. Harrison that this was my intention, he told me he had prepared a sermon for the occasion. I asked him what subject he had pitched upon, and I never shall forget his reply. He proposed, he said, to preach against *absolute monarchy*. It was impossible, I said, not to commend the judiciousness of his choice; as the times and the country in which our lot had fallen so particularly called on us to put our people on their guard against a danger into which they seemed so likely to fall. The fact was, I fancy, he had found such a sermon in Hoadly, and having transcribed it, shewed it to the Committee, by whom it was approved, as any and every thing was and would have been, however loose and weak, that but seemed to be against power and for liberty.

Mr. Addison, the Governor, and all the most judicious friends I had, looked over my sermon, and thought I had softened it down so, as that it might do good, and at least could not possibly give offence. In this and everything else that I now wrote, all that I could dare to hope to effect, was the restraining the body of the people from taking any active part; and the jet of my arguments was that in taking a part they could not be sure they were right and doing good; and so their truest wisdom as well as duty in so difficult a conjecture was, as the Prophet advised them, to *sit still*. And sadly as things went against loyalty and loyal men, I have the comfort

to reflect that some good was done by my efforts in their favour. I had some credit and character with my brethren of the
clergy, many of whom were thus restrained within the bounds
of duty. And as proof that many of the people were so restrained, I may mention that when members for the Provincial
Congress were to be chosen, as the measure was quite novel
and altogether unknown to our laws, I exhorted my people to
abstain from it, and not one of them attended. Out of the
whole county there were but thirteen electors; and in Annapolis there were but four. And it is a certain fact, of the truth
of which I at least am thoroughly convinced, that nine out of
ten of the people of America, properly so called, were adverse
to the revolt. But how shall an historian prove so extraordinary a fact, or expect to gain credit if he should prove it?

When the fast-day came I set off, accompanied by Mr.
Walter Dulany, since made a major in a Provincial Loyal
Regiment, and was at my church at least a quarter of an hour
before the usual time of beginning service. But behold, Mr.
Harrison was in the desk, and was expected also, as I was soon
told, to preach. This was not agreeable: but of how little sig-
nificance was this compared to what I next saw, viz. my
church filled with not less than 200 armed men, under the
command of Mr. Osborne Sprigg, who soon let me know I was
not to preach. I returned for answer that the pulpit was my
own, and as such I would use it; and that there was but one
way by which they could keep me out of it, and that was by
taking away my life. In church I managed to place myself so
as to have the command of the pulpit, and told my curate at his
peril not to attempt to dispossess me. Sundry messages were
sent, and applications made to me, to relinquish my purpose;
but as I knew it was my duty, and thought also that it was my
interest, not to relinquish it, I persisted. And so at the proper
time, with my sermon in one hand and a loaded pistol in the
other, like Nehemiah, I prepared to ascend the steps of the
pulpit, when behold, one of my friends (Mr. David Crawford
of Upper Marlborough) having got behind me, threw his arms

around mine and held me fast. He assured me on his honour he had both seen and heard the most positive orders given to twenty men picked out for the purpose to fire on me the moment I got into the pulpit, which therefore he never would permit me to do, unless I was stronger than he and two or three others who stood close to him. I entreated him and them to go with me into the pulpit, as my life seemed to myself to depend on my not suffering these outrageous people to carry their point; and I suppose we should all be safe while we were all together, for Mr. Crawford and those with him were rather against than for me in politics. In all these cases I argued that once to flinch was for ever to invite danger; and that as I could never be out of the reach of such men till I was out of the country, my only policy was, if possible, to intimidate them, as in some degree I had hitherto done. My well-wishers however prevailed — by force rather than by persuasion; and when I was down it is horrid to recollect what a scene of confusion ensued. A large party insisted I was right in claiming and using my own pulpit; but Sprigg and his company were now grown more violent, and soon managed so as to surround me, and to exclude every moderate man. Seeing myself thus circumstanced, it occurred to me that things seemed now indeed to be growing alarming, and that there was but one way to save my life. This was by seizing Sprigg, as I immediately did, by the collar, and with my cocked pistol in the other hand, assuring him that if any violence was offered to me I would instantly blow his brains out, as I most certainly would have done. I then told him that if he pleased he might conduct me to my horse, and I would leave them. This he did, and we marched together upwards of a hundred yards, I with one hand fastened in his collar and a pistol in the other, guarded by his whole company, whom he had the meanness to order to play on their drums the Rogues' March all the way we went, which they did. All farther that I could then do was to declare, as loud as I could speak, that he had now proved himself to be a complete coward and scoundrel.

Thus ended this dreadful day, which was a Thursday. On the Sunday following I again went to the same church, was again opposed, though more feebly than before, owing to an idea that I never would think of making another attempt. I preached the same sermon I should have preached on the Thursday, with some comments on the transactions of that day. After sermon, notice having been spread of my being at Church, a larger body assembled, and I found myself again surrounded and hustled. But placing my back against a pillar of the church, and being a little raised, I again began to bawl and to harangue, and again got off; so that this affray ended in a war of words.

CHAPTER 2   Congress Assessed

The pamphlet debate between future loyalists and revolutionaries began in 1774 over the decisions of the first Continental Congress. Joseph Galloway (c. 1731–1803) came from
a wealthy Pennsylvania family and had dominated the colony's
politics from his place as Speaker of the assembly. He presented the Congress with a plan for the federal union of the
colonies under the Crown. Later, Galloway, writing in the
third person, described his hopes and their frustration. The
failure of the plan convinced him that America was being
driven towards independence, and he became an eloquent
loyalist. He was the administrator of Philadelphia during the
British occupation, then went to England, indulged in pro-
lific pamphleteering, and was regarded as the leading loyalist
in exile.

Alexander Hamilton (1757–1804) was a student at King's
College, New York, at this time. Only seventeen, he sprang to
the defense of Congress, arguing that it was necessary to distinguish between its attack on the unjustifiable pretensions of
the British parliament and its respect for the virtues of the
British connection. To future loyalists such as the Rev. Samuel Seabury (1729–1796) Congress had definitely gone too far.
Seabury, born into one of the oldest Connecticut families, was
Episcopal minister in Westchester, New York. As "A West-

chester Farmer" (A. W. Farmer) he had penned an early
critique of Congress, inspiring young Hamilton to its defense.
Seabury's pamphlet quoted in this chapter was his riposte to
Hamilton. In November 1775, revolutionaries took Seabury
prisoner to New Haven and detained him for almost a year.
He then became chaplain in a loyalist corps, and in 1784 was
consecrated Bishop of Connecticut and Rhode Island, the first
bishop of the Episcopal Church in America.

JOSEPH GALLOWAY
*A Candid Examination of the Mutual Claims of Great-Britain and
the Colonies with a Plan of Accommodation on Constitutional
Principles.*

New York, Rivington, 1775, pp. 50–58

. . . Let us bring the case home to ourselves. The relation
between the sovereign authority and its members, bears a true
resemblance to that between parent and child. Their rights and
duties are similar. Should a child take umbrage at the conduct
of a parent, tell him that he was not his father, nor would he
consider himself, or act, as his child *on any terms;* ought the
parent to listen to such undutiful language, or could he be
justly censured for treating it with neglect, or even with contempt?

In order to prevail on the congress to desert their scheme of
independence, and to pursue those measures for restoring the
rights of America, which carried with them a prospect of success; a member of the congress . . . proposed a plan of union
between the two countries, which would have restored to the
colonists the full enjoyment of their rights. . . . He waited with
some patience to see whether any rational scheme of union
would be adopted by the congress, — determined to unite with
them in any measure which might tend to a reconciliation between the two countries; but he waited in vain: And when he
found them bewildered, perpetually changing their ground,

taking up principles one day, and shifting them the next, he thought it his duty, however little the prospect of success, to speak his sentiments with firmness, and to endeavour to show them the true line of their duty. After proving the necessity of a supreme authority over every member of the state, tracing the rights of the colonies to their origin, and fixing them on the most solid principles, and thence shewing the necessity of an union with the mother state, for the recovery of them; he introduced the plan with the resolve which precedes it. But before he delivered it to be read, he declared, that he was sensible it was not perfect; that knowing the fundamental principles of every system must be first settled, he had, to avoid perplexity, contented himself with only laying down the great out-lines of the union; and should they be approved of, that he had several propositions of lesser consequence to make, in order to render the system more complete. The plan read, and warmly seconded by several gentlemen of the first abilities, after a long debate, was so far approved as to be thought worthy of further consideration, and referred under a rule for that purpose, by a majority of the colonies. Under this promising aspect of things, and an expectation that the rule would have been regarded, or at least that something rational would take place to reconcile our unhappy differences, the member proposing it was weakly led to sign the non-importation agreement, although he had uniformly opposed it; but in this he was disappointed. — The measures of *independence and sedition,* were soon after preferred to those of *harmony and liberty;* and no arguments, however reasonable and just, could prevail on a majority of the colonies to desert them. The resolve, plan, and rule referring them to further consideration, so inconsistent with the measures now resolved on, were expunged from the minutes; with what view let America determine: And while the enemies to the gentleman who proposed them, are abusing him for offering [them] . . . they have copies of it in their pockets, industriously concealing it from the world. With what view can this be, but that their malevolent aspersions may take the greater effect? In justice therefore to the character of this gentleman, and that America may see and judge for itself, they are here offered to its consideration.

RESOLVED,

That the Congress will apply to his Majesty for a redress of grievances under which his faithful subjects in America labour; and assure him, that the Colonies hold in abhorrence the idea of being considered independent communities on the British government, and most ardently desire the establishment of a Political Union, not only among themselves, but with the Mother State, upon those principles of safety and freedom which are essential in the constitution of all free governments, and particularly that of the British Legislature; and as the Colonies from their local circumstances, cannot be represented in the Parliament of Great-Britain, they will humbly propose to his Majesty and his two Houses of Parliament, the following plan, under which the strength of the whole Empire may be drawn together on any emergency, the interest of both countries advanced, and the rights and liberties of America secured.

A PLAN OF A PROPOSED UNION BETWEEN
GREAT-BRITAIN AND THE COLONIES

That a British and American legislature, for regulating the administration of the general affairs of America, be proposed and established in America, including all the said colonies; within, and under which government, each colony shall retain its present constitution, and powers of regulating and governing its own internal police, in all cases whatever.

That the said government be administered by a President General, to be appointed by the King and a grand Council, to be chosen by the Representatives of the people of the several colonies, in their respective Assemblies, once in every three years.

That the several Assemblies shall choose members for the grand Council in the following proportions, viz.

New-Hampshire,
Massachusetts-Bay,
Rhode-Island,
Connecticut,
New-York,
New-Jersey,
Pennsylvania,

Delaware Counties,
Maryland,
Virginia,
North-Carolina,
South-Carolina,
    and
Georgia.

Who shall meet at the city of   for the first time, being called by the President-General, as soon as conveniently may be after his appointment.

That there shall be a new election of members for the Grand Council every three years; and on the death, removal or resignation of any member, his place shall be supplied by a new choice, at the next sitting of Assembly of the Colony he represented.

That the Grand Council shall meet once in every year, if they shall think it necessary, and oftner, if occasions shall require, at such time and place as they shall adjourn to, at the last preceding meeting, or as they shall be called to meet at, by the President-General, on any emergency.

That the grand Council shall have power to choose their Speaker, and shall hold and exercise all the like rights, liberties and privileges, as are held and exercised by and in the House of Commons of Great-Britain.

That the President-General shall hold his Office during the pleasure of the King, and his assent shall be requisite to all acts of the Grand Council, and it shall be his office and duty to cause them to be carried into execution.

That the President-General, by and with the advice and consent of the Grand-Council, hold and exercise all the legislative rights, powers, and authorities, necessary for regulating and administring all the general police and affairs of the colonies, in which Great-Britain and the colonies, or any of them, the colonies in general, or more than one colony, are in any manner concerned, as well civil and criminal as commercial.

That the said President-General and Grand Council, be an inferior and distinct branch of the British legislature, united and incorporated with it, for the aforesaid general purposes; and that any of the said general regulations may originate and be formed and digested, either in the Parliament of Great-Britain, or in the said Grand Council, and being prepared, transmitted to the other for their approbation or dissent; and that the assent of both shall be requisite to the validity of all such general acts or statutes.

That in time of war, all bills for granting aids to the crown, prepared by the Grand Council, and approved by the President General, shall be valid and passed into a law, without the assent of the British Parliament.

I shall not affirm that this plan is formed upon the most perfect principles of policy and government; but as it is an universally prevailing opinion, that the colonies cannot be represented in parliament: I know of none other which comes so near to them; and it is most evident, upon a due consideration of it, that the rights of America would have been fully restored, and her freedom effectually secured by it. For under it, no law can be binding on America, to which the people, by their representatives, have not previously given their consent: This is the essence of liberty, and what more would her people desire?

The author of this plan seems to have formed it on a comprehensive view of the regulations necessary to the interest and safety of the colonies. These he has divided into two classes: the first contain all such as the colony legislatures have a right to make, under the several constitutions, and to which they are adequate; these are to remain under their decisions; it being declared in the plan, that "each colony shall retain its present constitution and powers of regulating and governing its own internal police in all cases whatsoever." The others, which are to be the objects of the deliberations and decisions of the grand council, relate to the general interests and security of the colonies, and are absolutely necessary for those purposes; such laws for granting aids for the crown, and levying taxes in just and reasonable proportions in the colonies — for regulating a general paper currency, and the value of foreign coins, which ought in all good policy, to be established on funds equally solid, and ascertained at the same value; Laws for regulating and quartering troops, which may be necessary for their general protection; for settling disputes between the colonies, respecting their boundaries — with a variety of other matters that must naturally arise from the jarring interests of the colonies, which will continually encrease with the encrease of their wealth and commerce. And as to those, it must be owned, that the colony legislatures are not adequate; but that they must be made either by the parliament, or by some new establishment for those purposes. The authority of the first was objected to; and as to the second, or any other system of union, it being incompatible with the scheme of independence, it was not thought worthy of attention.

Objections were indeed made to this plan, which it may not be improper here to mention. It was said, "that the delegates did not come with authority to consent to a political union between the two countries." To which many arguments were opposed, to show that they had such authority or none; and concluded with desiring, that if that was, in the opinion of the members, the case, yet that the congress ought in justice to their country to digest and form one, and recommend it to their respective assemblies; by whom it would be presented with more constitutional propriety than by any other body of men. It was further said, "that the members of the grand council would be corrupted, and betray the interest of the colonies." To this it was answered — That if American virtue was not firm enough to maintain American liberty, it could be supported by no wisdom or policy whatever; but suppose the people to be in so corrupt a state; — yet as the election of the members was to be triennial, they might change them every 3 years, and the sums of money, necessary to bribe the new members, would be too great to be supplied: That the most sensible writers on the side of liberty agreed, if the parliament of England was triennial, it would destroy the system of corruption. Besides, to avoid all risque of the contrary, they might, by altering one word in the plan, make the election duennial, or annual, which must certainly remove the objection. A third objection was, That it deprived the colony legislatures of a part of their rights: To which it was replied, that a colony legislature is capable of passing laws to regulate its internal police; but not adequate to any general regulation, not even in the necessary one of taxation. That there is no proposition more just, than that every colony, as a member of the state, ought to be obliged to contribute towards the defence of the whole, in proportion to the property and wealth which each colony possesses. That this is a primary consideration in every society; and that no one colony had a constitutional power to obtain the amount and value of the property of the others, by which to ascertain its proportion. Nor was there any authority whatever, save the British Parliament, to compel refractory colonies to do their reasonable duty, in this or any other general measure; and that this plan was so far from diminishing the rights of any colony legislature, that it extended them; by giving to each a new jurisdiction, to decide upon regulations which relate to the general police of all the colonies.

Such was the plan laid before the congress, the objections against, and the arguments in favour of it. They are here laid before the public, to enable them to judge for themselves, whether, as a representation in parliament, is generally supposed to be impracticable, any thing more consistent with their safety could have been adopted.

ALEXANDER HAMILTON

A friend to America, A Full Vindication of the Measures of the Congress, from the Calumnies of their Enemies, by A. W. Farmer, Author of Free Thoughts ....

New York, Rivington, 1774

FRIENDS AND COUNTRYMEN

It was hardly to be expected that any man could be so presumptuous, as openly to controvert the equity, wisdom, and authority of the measures, adopted by the congress: an assembly truly respectable on every account! — Whether we consider the characters of the men, who composed it; the number, and dignity of their constituents, or the important ends for which they were appointed. But, however improbable such a degree of presumption might have seemed, we find there are some, in whom it exists. Attempts are daily making to diminish the influence of their decisions, and prevent the salutary effects, intended by them. — The impotence of such insidious efforts is evident from the general indignation they are treated with; so that no material ill-consequences can be dreaded from them. But lest they should have a tendency to mislead, and prejudice the minds of a few; it cannot be deemed altogether useless to bestow some notice upon them.

And first, let me ask these restless spirits, whence arises that violent antipathy they seem to entertain, not only to the natural rights of mankind; but to common sense and common modesty. That they are enemies to the natural rights of mankind is manifest, because they wish to see one part of their species enslaved by another. That they have an invincible aversion to common sense is apparent in many respects: They endeavour to persuade us, that the absolute sovereignty of Parliament does not imply our absolute slavery; . . . The only distinction between freedom and slavery consists in this: In the former state, a man is governed by the laws to which he has given his consent, either in person, or by his representative; in the latter, he is governed by the will of another. In the one case his life and property are his own, in the other, they depend upon the pleasure of the master. It is easy to discern which of these two states is preferable. No man in his sense can hesitate in choosing to be free, rather than a slave.

That Americans are intitled to freedom, is incontestible upon every rational principle. All men have one common original: they participate in one common nature, and consequently have one common right. No reason can be assigned why one man should exercise any power, or pre-eminence over his fellow creatures more than another; unless they have voluntarily vested him with it. Since then, Americans have not by any act of their's impowered the British Parliament to make laws for them, it follows they can have no just authority to do it.

Besides the clear voice of natural justice in this respect, the fundamental principles of the English constitution are in our favour. It has been repeatedly demonstrated, that the idea of legislation, or taxation, when the subject is not represented, is inconsistent with *that*. Nor is this all, our charters, the express conditions on which our progenitors relinquished their native countries, and came to settle in this, preclude every claim of ruling and taxing us without our assent.

Every subterfuge that sophistry has been able to invent, to evade or obscure this truth, has been refuted by the most conclusive reasonings; so that we may pronounce it a matter of undeniable certainty, that the pretensions of Parliament are contradictory to the law of nature, subversive of the British constitution, and destructive of the faith of the most solemn compacts.

What then is the subject of our controversy with the mother country? — It is this, whether we shall preserve that security to our lives and properties, which the law of nature, the genius of the British constitution, and our charters afford us; or whether we shall resign them into the hands of the British House of Commons, which is no more privileged to dispose of them than the Grand Mogul? — What can actuate those men, who labour to delude any of us into an opinion, that the object of contention between the parent state and the colonies is only three pence duty upon tea? or that the commotions in America originate in a plan, formed by some turbulent men to erect it into a republican government? The parliament claims a right to tax us in all cases whatsoever: Its late acts are in virtue of that claim. — How ridiculous then is it to affirm, that we are quarrelling for the trifling sum of three pence a pound on tea; when it is evidently the principle against which we contend.

The design of electing members to represent us in general congress, was, that the wisdom of America might be collected in devising the most proper and expedient means to repel this atrocious invasion of our rights. It has been accordingly done. Their decrees are binding upon all, and demand a religious observance. . . .

*   *   *

When the political salvation of any community is depending, it is incumbent upon those who are set up as its guardians,

to embrace such measures as have justice, vigour, and a probability of success to recommend them: If instead of this, they
take those methods which are in themselves feeble, and little
likely to succeed; and may, through a defect in vigour, involve
the community in still greater danger; they may be justly considered as its betrayers. It is not enough in times of eminent
peril to use only possible means of preservation: Justice and
sound policy dictate the use of probable means.

The only scheme of opposition, suggested by those, who
have been, and are averse from a non-importation and non-
exportation agreement, is, by REMONSTRANCE and PETITION.
The authors and abettors of this scheme, have never been able
to *invent* a single argument to prove the likelihood of its succeeding. . . .

*   *   *

Should Americans submit to become the vassals of their
fellow-subjects in Great Britain, their yoke will be peculiarly
grievous and intolerable. A vast majority of mankind is intirely biassed by motives of self-interest. Most men are glad
to remove any burthens off themselves, and place them upon
the necks of their neighbours. We cannot therefore doubt, but
that the British Parliament, with a view to the ease and advantage of itself, and its constituents, would oppress and grind the
Americans as much as possible. Jealousy would concur with
selfishness; and for fear of the future independence of America,
if it should be permitted to rise to too great a height of splendor and opulence, every method would be taken to drain it of
its wealth and restrain its prosperity. We are already suspected
of aiming at independence, and that is one principal cause of
the severity we experience. The same cause will always operate against us, and produce an uniform severity of treatment.

The evils which may flow from the execution of our measures, if we consider them with respect to their extent and
duration, are comparatively nothing. In all human probability
they will scarcely be felt. Reason and experience teach us,

that the consequences would be too fatal to Great Britain to admit of delay. There is an immense trade between her and the colonies. The revenues arising from thence are prodigious. The consumption of her manufactures in these colonies supplies the means of subsistence to a vast number of her most useful inhabitants. The experiment we have made heretofore, shews us of how much importance our commercial connexion is to her; and gives us the highest assurance of obtaining immediate redress by suspending it.

From these considerations it is evident, that she must do something decisive. She must either listen to our complaints, and restore us to a peaceful enjoyment of our violated rights; or she must exert herself to enforce her despotic claims by fire and sword. To imagine she would prefer the latter, implies a charge of the very grossest infatuation of madness itself. Our numbers are very considerable; the courage of Americans has been tried and proved. Contests for liberty have ever been found the most bloody, implacable and obstinate. The disciplined troops Great Britain could send against us, would be but few. Our superiority in number would overbalance our inferiority in discipline. It would be a hard, if not an impracticable task to subjugate us by force.

Besides, while Great Britain was engaged in carrying on an unnatural war against us, her commerce would be in a state of decay. Her revenues would be decreasing. An armament, sufficient to enslave America, would put her to an insupportable expence.

She would be laid open to the attacks of foreign enemies. Ruin, like a deluge, would pour in from every quarter. After lavishing her blood and treasure to reduce us to a state of vassalage, she would herself become a prey to some triumphant neighbour.

These are not imaginary mischiefs. The colonies contain above three millions of people. Commerce flourishes with the most rapid progress throughout them. This commerce Great-Britain has hitherto regulated to her own advantage. Can we think the annihilation of so exuberant a source of wealth, a matter of trifling import. On the contrary, must it not be productive of the most disastrous effects? It is evident it must. It is equally evident, that the conquest of so numerous a people, armed in the animating cause of liberty could not be accomplished without an inconceivable expence of blood and treasure.

We cannot therefore suspect Great-Britain to be capable of such frantic extravagance as to hazard these dreadful consequences; without which she must necessarily desist from her unjust pretensions, and leave us in the undisturbed possession of our privileges.

Those, who affect to ridicule the resistance America might make to the military force of Great-Britain, and represent its humiliation as a matter the most easily to be achieved, betray, either a mind clouded by the most irrational prejudices, or a total ignorance of human nature. However, it must be the wish of every honest man never to see a trial.

S A M U E L   S E A B U R Y

A. W. Farmer, A View of the Controversy between Great Britain and her Colonies: including a Mode of determining their present Disputes, Finally and Effectually, and of preventing all future Contentions, in A Letter to the Author of A Full Vindication of the Measures of the Congress. . . .

New York, Rivington, 1774, pp. 8–11, 14–19, 21, 32–33

I wish you had explicitly declared to the public your ideas of the *natural rights of mankind.* Man in a *state of nature* may be considered as perfectly free from all restraints of law and government: And then the *weak* must submit to the *strong.* From such a state, I confess, I have a violent aversion. I think the form of government we lately enjoyed a much more eligible state to live in: And cannot help regretting our having *lost* it, by the *equity, wisdom,* and *authority* of the Congress, who have introduced in the room of it, confusion and violence; where all must submit to the power of a mob.

You have taken some pains to prove what would readily have been granted you — that *liberty* is a very *good* thing, and *slavery* a very *bad* thing. But then I must think that liberty under a *King, Lords* and *Commons* is as good as liberty under a republican Congress: And that slavery under a republican Congress is as bad, at least, as slavery under a *King, Lords* and *Commons:* And upon the whole, that *liberty* under the supreme authority and protection of Great-Britain, is infinitely preferable to *slavery* under an American Congress. I will also agree with you, "that Americans are entitled to freedom." I will go further: I will own and acknowledge that not only *Americans,* but *Africans, Europeans, Asiaticks,* all men, of all countries and degrees, of all sizes and complexions, have a right to as much freedom as is consistent with security of civil society: And I hope you will not think me "an enemy to the *natural* rights of mankind" because I cannot wish them more. We must however remember, that more liberty may, without inconvenience, be allowed to individuals in a small government, than can be admitted of in a large empire.

But when you assert that "since then, Americans have not by any act of theirs impowered the British Parliament to make laws for them, it follows they can have no just authority to do it" you advance a position subversive of that dependence which all colonies must, from their very nature, have on the Mother Country. By the British Parliament, I suppose you mean the supreme legislative authority, the King, Lords, and Commons, because no other authority in England has a right to make laws to bind the kingdom, and consequently no authority to make laws to bind the colonies. In this sense I shall understand, and use the phrase *British Parliament.*

Now the dependence of the colonies on the Mother Country has ever been acknowledged. It is an impropriety of speech to talk of an independent colony. The words *independency* and *colony*, convey contradictory ideas: much like *killing* and *sparing*. As soon as a colony becomes independent on its parent state it ceases to be any longer a colony; just as when you *kill* a sheep, you cease to *spare* him. The British colonies make a part of the British empire. As parts of the body they must be subject to the general laws of the body. To talk of a colony independent of the Mother Country, is no better sense than to talk of a limb independent of the body to which it belongs.

In every government there must be a supreme, absolute authority lodged somewhere. In arbitrary governments this power is in the monarch; in aristocratical governments, in the nobles; in democratical governments in the people; or the deputies of their electing. Our own government being a mixture of all these kinds, the supreme authority is vested in the King, Nobles and People, in the King, House of Lords, and House of Commons elected by the people. This supreme authority extends as far as the British dominions extend. To suppose a part of the British dominions which is not subject to the power of the British legislature, is no better sense than to suppose a country, at one in the same time to be, and not to be a part of the British dominions. If therefore the colony of New-York be a part of the British dominions the colony of New-York is subject, and dependent on the supreme legislative authority of Great Britain.

Legislation is not an inherent right in the colonies. Many colonies have been established, and subsisted long without it. The Roman colonies had no legislative authority. It was not till the later period of their republic that the privileges of Roman citizens, among which that of voting in the assemblies of the people at Rome was a principal one, were extended to the inhabitants of Italy. All the laws of the empire were enacted at Rome. Neither their colonies, nor conquered countries had anything to do with legislation.

The position that we are bound by no laws to which we have not consented, either by ourselves, or our representatives, is a novel position, unsupported by any authoritative record of the British Constitution, ancient or modern. It is republican in its very nature, and tends to the utter subversion of the English monarchy.

This position has arisen from an artful change of terms. To say that an Englishman is not bound by any laws, but those to which the representatives of the nation have given their consent, is to say what is true: But to say that an Englishman is bound by no laws but those to which *he* hath consented in person, or by *his* representative, is saying what never was true, and never can be true. A great part of the people in England have no vote in the choice of representatives, and therefore are governed by laws to which they never consented either by *themselves* or by *their* representatives.

The right of colonists to exercise a legislative power, is no natural right. They derive it not from nature, but from the indulgence or grant of the parent state, whose subjects they were when the colony was settled, and by whose permission and assistance they made the settlement.

Upon supposition that every English colony enjoyed a legislative power independent of the parliament; and that the parliament has no just authority to make laws to bind them, this absurdity will follow — that there is no power in the British empire, which has authority to make laws for the whole empire; i.e. we have an empire, without government; or which amounts to the same thing, we have a government which has no supreme power. All our colonies are independent of each other: Suppose them independent of the British Parliament, — what power do you leave to govern the whole? None at all. You split and divide the empire into a number of petty insignificant states. This is the direct, the necessary tendency of refusing submission to acts of Parliament. Every man who can see one inch beyond his nose, must see this consequence. And every man who endeavours to accelerate the independency of the colonies on the British Parliament, endeavours to accelerate the ruin of the British empire.

To talk of being liege subjects to King GEORGE, while we disavow the authority of Parliament is another piece of whiggish nonsense. I love my King as well as any whig in America or England either, and am as ready to yield him all lawful submission: But while I submit to the King, I submit to the authority of the laws of the state, whose guardian the King is. The difference between a good and bad subject, is only this, that the one obeys, the other transgresses the law. The difference between a loyal subject and a rebel, is, that the one yields obedience to, and faithfully supports the supreme authority of the state, and the other endeavours to overthrow it. If we obey the laws of the King, we obey the laws of the Parliament. If we disown the authority of the Parliament, we disown the authority of the King. There is no median without ascribing powers to the King which the constitution knows nothing of: — without making him superior to the laws, and setting him above all restraint. These are some of the ridiculous absurdities of American whiggism. . . .

*   *   *

If it be said, that admitting the foregoing reasoning and authorities, yet the right of taxation will not follow, let it be considered, that in every government, *legislation* and *taxation*, or the right of raising a revenue, must be conjoined. If you divide them, you weaken, and finally destroy the government; for no government can long subsist without power to raise the supplies necessary for its defence and administration. It has been proved, that the supreme authority of the British empire extends over all the dominions that compose the empire. The power, or right of the British Parliament to raise such a revenue as is necessary for the defence and support of the British government, in all parts of the British dominion, is therefore incontestable. For if no government can subsist without a power to raise the revenues necessary for its support, then, in fact, no government can extend any further than its power of raising such a revenue extends. If therefore the British Parliament has no power to raise a revenue in the colonies, it has no government over the colonies, i.e., no government can support itself. The burthen of supporting its government over the colonies must lie upon the other parts of the empire. But this is unreasonable. Government implies, not only a power of making and enforcing *laws*, but defence and protection. Now protection implies tribute. Those that share in the protection of any government, are in reason and duty, bound to maintain and support the government that protects them: Otherwise they destroy their own protection; or else they throw an unjust burthen on their fellow-subjects, which they ought to bear in common with them. While therefore the colonies are under the British government, and share in its protection, the British government has a right to raise, and they are in reason and duty bound to pay, a reasonable and proportionable part of the expense of its administration.

There are but two objections that can reasonably be made to what has been said upon this subject. The first is, that if the British Parliament has a right to make laws to bind the whole empire, our assemblies become useless. But a little consideration will remove this difficulty.

Our assemblies, from the very nature of things, can have but a legated, subordinate, and local authority of legislation. Their power of making laws in conjunction with the other branches of the legislature, cannot extend beyond the limits of the province to which they belong. Their authority must be subordinate to the supreme authority of the nation, or there is *imperium in imperio:* two sovereign authorities in the same state; which is a contradiction. Every thing that relates to the internal policy and government of the province which they represent comes properly before them; whether they be matters of law or revenue. But all laws relative to the empire in general or to all the colonies conjunctively, or which regulates the trade of any particular colony, in order to make it compatible with the general good of the whole empire, must be left to the parliament. There is no other authority which has a *right* to make such regulations, or *weight* sufficient to carry them into execution.

Our Assemblies are also the true, proper, legal guardians of our *rights, privileges* and *liberties.* If any laws of the British parliament are thought oppressive; or if, in the administration of the British government, any unnecessary or unreasonable burthen be laid upon us, *they* are the proper persons to seek for redress: And they are the most likely to succeed, they have the legal and constitutional means in their hands. They are the *real* not the *pretended* representatives of the people. They are bodies known to and acknowledged by the public laws of the empire. Their representations will be attended to, and their remonstrances heard. . . .

*   *   *

The other objection to what has been said upon the legislative authority of the British Parliament, is this: That if the Parliament have authority to make laws to bind the whole empire; — to regulate the trade of the whole empire; — and to raise a revenue upon the whole empire; then we have nothing that we can call our own: — By the same authority that they can take a penny, they can take a pound, or all we have got.

Let it be considered, that no scheme of human policy can be so contrived and guarded, but that something must be left to the integrity, prudence, and wisdom of those who govern. We are apt to think, and I believe justly, that the British constitution is the best scheme of government now subsisting: the rights and liberties of the people are better secured by it, than by any other system now subsisting. And yet we find that the rights and liberties of Englishmen may be infringed by wicked and ambitious men. This will ever be the case, even after human sagacity has exerted its utmost ability. This is, however, no argument, that we should not secure ourselves as well as we can. It is rather an argument, that we should use our utmost endeavour to guard against the attempts of ambition or avarice.

A great part of the people in England, a considerable number of people in this province, are bound by laws, and taxed without their consent, or the consent of their representatives: for representatives they have none, unless the absurd position of a *virtual* representation be admitted. These people may object to the present mode of government. They may say, that they have nothing that they can call their own. That if they may be taxed a penny without their consent, they may be taxed a pound; and so on. You will think it a sufficient security to these people, that the representatives of the nation or province cannot hurt *them*, without hurting themselves; because, they cannot tax *them*, without taxing themselves. This security however may not be so effectual as at first may be imagined. The rich are never taxed so much in proportion to their estates as the poor: And even an equal proportion of that tax which a rich man can easily pay, may be a heavy burthen to a poor man. But the same security that these people have against being ruined by the representatives of the nation, or province where they live; the same security have we against being ruined by the British Parliament. They cannot hurt us without hurting themselves. The principal profits of our trade center in England. If they lay unnecessary or oppressive burthens on it; or any ways restrain it, so as to injure us, they will soon feel the effect, and very readily remove the cause. If this security is thought insufficient, let us endeavour to obtain a more effectual one. Let it however be remembered, that this security has been thought, and felt sufficient till within a short period; and very probably, a prudent management, and a temperate conduct on our part, would have made it permanently effectual.

But the colonies have become so considerable by the increase of their inhabitants and commerce, and by the improvement of their lands, that they seem incapable of being governed
in the same lax and precarious manner as formerly. They are
arrived to that mature state of manhood which requires a
different, and more exact policy of ruling, than was necessary
in their infancy and childhood. They want, and are entitled
to, a fixed determinate constitution of their own. A constitution which shall unite them firmly with Great Britain, and
with one another; — which shall mark out the line of British
supremacy, and colonial dependence, giving on the one hand
full force to the supreme authority of the nation over all its
dominions and on the other, securing effectually the rights,
liberty, and property of the colonists. — This is an event devoutly to be wished, by all good men; and which all ought to
labour to obtain by all prudent, and probable means. Without
obtaining this, it is idle to talk of obtaining a redress of the
grievances complained of. They naturally, they necessarily
result from the relation which we at present stand in to Great
Britain. . . .

*   *   *

I will here, Sir, venture to deliver my sentiments upon the
line that ought to be drawn between the supremacy of Great-
Britain, and the dependency of the Colonies. And I shall do
it with the more boldness, because I know it to be agreeable
to the opinions of many of the warmest advocates for America
both in England and in the colonies, in the time of the Stamp
Act. — I imagine that if all internal taxation be vested in our
own legislatures, and the right of regulating trade by duties,
bounties, &c be left in the power of the Parliament; and also
the right of enacting all general laws for the good of all the
colonies, that we shall have all the security for our rights, liberties and property, which human policy can give us: The dependence of the colonies on the Mother Country will be fixed
on a firm foundation; the sovereign authority of Parliament,

over all the dominions of the empire will be established, and the mother-country and all her colonies will be knit together, in ONE GRAND, FIRM, AND COMPACT BODY. . . .

*   *   *

Now what concessions can Great Britain make, that would satisfy you and your party? She has it not in her power to make any — were she even desirous of doing it, and willing to sacrifice her own honour and dignity, to gratify your humours. She has no choice but to declare the colonies independent states, or to try the force of arms, in order to bring them to a sense of their duty. This is the wretched state to which your adored Congress have reduced us, and to which they deserve the *curse* of every inhabitant of America. No alternative is left us, but either to renounce *their* measures, or to plunge head-long into rebellion and civil war. . . .

*   *   *

You affect on every occasion to display "the omnipotency and all-sufficiency" of those colonies which have entered into *the* solemn league and covenant against Great-Britain. You mention the considerable numbers of their men — 400,000, I think your *Generalissimo* rates them at their valour, and bloody disposition in the cause of liberty. I wish you had told us what resources the colonies have, to pay, cloath, arm, feed these considerable numbers: — who are to levy the taxes necessary to defray the expence of these articles. Whether that is to be the business of the next congress.

On the other hand you always speak of Great-Britain, as of some pitiful state just sinking into obscurity. — You mention the small number of her troops in America; — the decay of her commerce; — the decrease of her revenue; — her luxury, — national debt, &c. — the danger lest the neighbouring states should all fall upon her, should she venture in a military way to spend across the Atlantic. . . . Do you think, Sir, that Great Britain is like an old, wrinkled, withered, wornout hag, whom every jackanapes that truants along the streets may insult with impunity? — You will find her a vigorous matron, just approaching a green old age; and with spirit and strength sufficient to chastise her undutiful and rebellious children. Your measures have as yet produced none of the effects you look for: Great Britain is not as yet intimidated. She has already a considerable fleet and army in America: More ships and troops are expected in the spring: Every appearance indicates a design in her to support her claim with vigour. You may call it *infatuation, madness, frantic extravagance,* to hazard so small a number of troops as she can spare, against the thousands of New England. Should the dreadful contest once begin — But God forbid! Save Heavenly Father! Oh save my country from perdition!

Consider, Sir, is it right to risk the valuable blessings of property, liberty and life, to the single chance of war? Of the worst kind of war — a civil war? a civil war founded on rebellion. Without ever attempting the peaceable mode of accommodation? Without ever asking a redress of our complaints, from the only power on earth who can redress them? When disputes happen between nations independent of each other, they first attempt to settle them by their ambassadors; they seldom run hastily to war, till they have tried what can be done by treaty and mediation. I would make many more concessions to a parent, than were justly due to him, rather than engage with him in a duel. But we are rushing into a war with our parent state, without offering the least concession; without even deigning to propose an accommodation. You, Sir, have employed your pen, and exerted your abilities, in vindicating and recommending measures which you know must, if persisted in, have a direct tendency to produce and accelerate the dreadful event.

CHAPTER 3

Two Loyalist
Views

Despite the early fears of men such as Galloway and Seabury, the issues that separated loyalist and revolutionary remained ill-defined throughout 1775. Later generations may have been able to discern a sequence of events leading to independence, but this was not necessarily clear to those living at the time. For one thing, many who became loyalists took the same hostile view of Parliament's actions as did the future revolutionaries. In these circumstances it proved difficult to organise the sentiment of loyalty, to defend without knowing what stood in need of defense.

Daniel Leonard (1740–1829) hoped to arouse his countrymen to a full awareness of what was taking place. Leonard was a member of an old established Massachusetts family that had found prosperity as ironmasters. A Harvard graduate and lawyer, he had been appointed king's attorney for Bristol county in 1769, and in the following year made his debut in the General Court as a critic of royal policy. However, in 1774, he was one of the councilors appointed by the crown after the revocation of Massachusetts' charter. He was forced to flee his home for Boston where, safe within British lines, he wrote seventeen letters for the *Massachusetts Gazette*. He argued that the development of opposition to Britain had been so gradual that many had reached the brink of independence without fully realising what they had done. Considering the past benevolence of Great Britain, such a crisis could only have arisen through general ignorance of what was at stake. Even the Continental Congress had departed from its original laudable aims and been made to serve the advocates of independence. When this minority was recognised in its true colors, then the good sense of the public would reassert itself. Alas for such hopes! Leonard joined the British in their retreat from Boston to Halifax; thence he went to Bermuda as chief justice. From 1815 to his death he lived and practiced law in London.

William Eddis (born 1745) was a copybook loyalist caught in the classic loyalist quandary: how far could he afford to sympathise with specific colonial grievances without being caught up in the general resistance movement? A recent arrival from England, Eddis was secretary to Governor Eden of Maryland, commissioner of the loan office and surveyor of the customs. In a letter to the *Maryland Gazette* he publicly accepted that Parliament had no right to tax the colonies, and concentrated on the least dangerous way to obtain redress of grievance; but privately he confessed that he was not even sure in his own mind how far Britain's authority extended over the colonies. Eddis stayed on in the new state of Maryland until 1777, assisting the government's investigation of the loan office, and then returned to England. In 1792 he published his reminiscences, privately, in the form of letters to an unspecified correspondent.

DANIEL   LEONARD
Massachusettensis, *Boston, Mills and Hicks*
1775, 3–9, 102–103, 106–110

To THE INHABITANTS OF THE PROVINCE OF
THE MASSACHUSETTS-BAY

When a people, by what means soever, are reduced to such a situation, that everything they hold dear, as men and citizens,

is at stake, it is not only excuseable, but even praiseworthy for
an individual to offer to the public anything that he may think
has a tendency to ward off the impending danger; nor should
he be restrained from an apprehension that what he may offer
will be unpopular, any more than a physician should be restrained from prescribing a salutary medicine through fear it
might be unpalatable to his patient.

The press, when open to all the parties and influenced by
none, is a salutary engine in a free state, perhaps a necessary
one to preserve the freedom of that state; but, when a party
has gained the ascendancy so far as to become the licensers of
the press, either by an act of government, or by playing off
the resentment of the populace against printers and authors,
the press itself becomes an engine of oppression or licentiousness, and is as pernicious to society as otherwise it would be
beneficial. It is too true to be denied that ever since the origin
of our controversy with Great Britain, the press, in this town
has been much devoted to the partizans of liberty; they have
been indulged in publishing what they pleased, *fas vel nefas*,
while little has been published on the part of government; the
effect this must have had upon the minds of the people in
general is obvious; they must have formed their opinion upon
a particular view of the subject, and of course, it must have
been to some degree erroneous: In short, the changes have
been rung so often upon oppression, tyranny and slavery,
that, whether sleeping or waking, they are continually vibrat-
ing in our ears; and it is now high time to ask ourselves
whether we have not been deluded by sound only.

My dear countrymen, let us divest ourselves of prejudice,
take a view of our present wretched situation, contrast it with
our former happy one, carefully investigate the cause, and
industriously seek some means to escape the evils we now feel,
and prevent those that we have reason to expect.

We have been so long advancing to our present state, and by
such gradations, that perhaps many of us are insensible of our
true state and real danger. Should you be told that acts of
high treason are flagrant through the country, that a great part

of the province is in actual rebellion, would you believe it true? Should you not deem the person asserting it an enemy to the province? Nay, should you not spurn him from you with indignation? Be calm, my friends, it is necessary to know the worst of a disease, to enable us to provide an effectual remedy. Are not the bands of society cut asunder, and the sanctions that hold man to man trampled upon? Can any of us recover a debt, or obtain compensation for an injury, by law? Are not many persons, whom once we respected and revered, driven from their homes and families, and forced to fly to the army for protection, for no other reason but their having accepted commissions under our King? Is not civil government dissolved? Some have been made to believe that nothing short of attempting the life of the King, or fighting his troops, can amount to high treason or rebellion. If, reader, you are one of those, apply to an honest lawyer (if such an one can be found) and enquire what kind of offence it is for a number of men to assemble, armed and forcibly to obstruct the course of justice, even to prevent the King's courts from being held at their stated terms; for a body of people to seize upon the King's provincial revenue; I mean the monies collected by virtue of grants made by the general court to his Majesty for the support of his government within this province; for a body of men to assemble without being called by authority, and to pass governmental acts, or for a number of people to take the militia out of the hands of the King's representative, or to form a new militia, or to raise men and appoint offices for a public purpose, without the order or permission of the King or his representative; or for a number of men to take to their arms, and march with a professed design of opposing the King's troops; ask, reader, of such a lawyer, what is the crime, and what the punishment; and if per chance thou art one that hast been active in these things, and art not insensibility itself, his answer will harrow up thy soul.

I assure you, my friends, I would not that this conduct should be told beyond the borders of this province; I wish it

were consigned to perpetual oblivion; but also, it is too notori-
ous to be concealed, our news-papers have already published
it to the world, we can neither prevent nor conceal it. The
shaft is already sped, and the utmost exertion is necessary to
prevent the blow. We already feel the effects of anarchy;
mutual confidence, affection and tranquility, those sweeteners
of human life, are succeeded by distrust, hatred and wild
uproars; the useful arts of agriculture and commerce are
neglected for caballing, mobbing this or the other man, because he acts, speaks or is suspected of thinking different from
the prevailing sentiments of the times, in purchasing arms and
forming a militia; O height of madness! With a professed
design of opposing Great-Britain. I suspect many of us have
been induced to join in these measures, or but faintly to oppose
them, from an apprehension that Great-Britain would not or
could not exert herself sufficiently to subdue America. Let us
consider this matter: However closely we may hug ourselves
in the opinion that the Parliament has no right to tax or legis-
late for us, the people of England hold the contrary opinion
as firmly; they tell us we are a part of the British empire; that
every state from the nature of government must have a supreme uncontrolable power coextensive with the empire itself;
and that, that power is vested in parliament. It is as unpopular
to deny this doctrine in Great-Britain as it is to assert it in
the colonies; so there is but little probability of serving ourselves at this day by our ingenious distinctions between a right
of legislation for one purpose and not for another. We have
bid them defiance, and the longest sword must carry it, unless
we change our measures. Mankind are the same in all parts of
the world; the same fondness for dominion that presides in
the breast of an American, actuates the breast of an European.
If the colonies are not a part of the British empire already, and
subject to the supreme authority of the state, Great-Britain
will make them so. Had we been prudent enough to confine
our opposition within certain limits, we might have stood some
chance of succeeding once more, but alas we have passed the

Rubicon. It is now universally said and believed, in England, that if this opportunity of reclaiming the colonies, and reducing them to a sense of their duty is lost, they in truth will be dismembered from the empire, and become as distinct a state from Great-Britain as Hanover; that is, although they may continue their allegiance to the person of the King, they will owe none to the imperial crown of Great-Britain, nor yield obedience to any of her laws but such as they shall think proper to adopt. Can you indulge the thought one moment, that Great-Britain will consent to this? For what has she protected and defended the colonies against the maritime powers of Europe from their first British settlement to this day? For what did she purchase New-York of the Dutch? For what was she so lavish of her best blood and treasure in the conquest of Canada and other territories in America? Was it to raise up a rival state, or to enlarge her own empire? Or if the consideration of empire was out of the question, what security can she have of our trade, where once she has lost our obedience? I mention these things, my friends, that you may know how people reason upon the subject in England; and to convince you that you are much deceived if you imagine that Great-Britain will accede to the claims of the colonies, she will as soon conquer New England as Ireland or Canada, if either of them revolted, and by arms, if the milder influences of government prove ineffectual. Perhaps you are as fatally mistaken in another respect, I mean as to the power of Great-Britain to conquer; but can any of you, that think soberly upon the matter, be so deluded as to believe that Great-Britain, who so lately carried her arms with success to every part of the globe, triumphed over the united powers of France and Spain, and whose fleets give law to the ocean, is unable to conquer us? Should the colonies unite in a war against Great-Britain (which by the way is not a supposeable case) the colonies south of Pennsylvania would be unable to furnish any men; they have not more than is necessary to govern their numerous slaves, and to defend themselves against the Indians. I will suppose that the northern colonies can furnish as many, and indeed more men than can be used to advantage, but have you arms fit for a campaign? If you have arms, have you military stores, or can you procure them? When this war is proclaimed, all supplies from foreign ports will be cut off. Have you money to maintain the war? Or had you all those things, some others are still wanting, which are absolutely necessary to encounter regular troops, that is discipline, and that subordination whereby each can command all below him from a general officer to the lowest subaltern; these you neither have nor can have in such a war. It is well known that the provincials in the late war were never brought to a proper discipline, though they had the example of the regular troops to encourage, and the martial law to enforce it. We all know, notwithstanding the province law for regulating the militia, it was under little more command than what the officers could obtain from treating and humouring the common soldiers; what then can be expected from such an army as you will bring into the field, if you bring any, each one a politician, puffed up with his own opinion, and preening himself second to none? Can any of you command ten thousand such men? Can you punish the disobedient? Can all your wisdom direct their strength, courage or activity to any given point? Would not the least disappointment or unfavourable aspect cause a general dereliction of the service? Your new-fangled militia have already given us a *specimen* of their future conduct. In some of their companies, they have already chosen two, in others three sets of officers, and are as dissatisfied with the last choice as the first. I do not doubt the natural bravery of my countrymen, all men would act the same part in the same situation. Such is the army with which you are to oppose the most powerful nation upon the globe. An experienced officer would rather take his chance with five thousand British troops, than with fifty thousand such militia. I have hitherto confined my observations to the war within the interior parts of the colonies, let us now turn our eyes to our extensive coasts, and that we find wholly at the mercy of Great-Britain; our trade, fishery, navigation and maritime towns taken from us the very day the war is proclaimed. Inconceivably shocking the scene; if we turn our views to the wilderness, our back settlements a prey to our ancient enemy, the Canadians, whose wounds received from us in the late war will bleed afresh at the prospect of revenge, and to the numerous tribes of savages, whose tender mercies are cruelties; thus with the British navy in the front, Canadians and savages in the rear, a regular army in the midst, we must be certain that whenever the sword of civil war is unsheathed, devastation will pass through our land like a whirlwind, our houses be burnt to ashes, our fair possessions laid waste, and he that falls by the sword will be happy in escaping a more ignominious death.

I have hitherto gone upon a supposition that all the colonies from Nova-Scotia to Georgia would unite in the war against Great-Britain, but I believe if we consider coolly upon the matter, we shall find no reason to expect any assistance out of New-England; if so, there will be no arm stretched out to save us, New-England, or perhaps this self-devoted province will fall alone the unpitied victim of its own folly, and furnish the world with one more instance of the fatal consequence of rebellion.

I have as yet said nothing of the differences in sentiment amongst ourselves; upon a superficial view we might imagine that this province was nearly unanimous, but the case is far different; a very considerable part of the men of property in this province, are at this day firmly attached to the cause of government; bodies of men compelling persons to disavow their sentiments, to resign commissions, or to subscribe leagues and covenants, have wrought no change in their sentiments, it has only attached them more closely to government, and caused them to wish more fervently, and to pray more devoutly for its restoration; these and thousands beside, if they fight at all, will fight under the banners of loyalty. I can assure you that associations are now forming in several parts of this province for the support of His Majesty's government and mutual defence; and let me tell you, whenever the royal standard shall be set up, there will be such a flocking to it, as will astonish the most obdurate. And now, in God's name, what is it that has brought us to the brink of destruction? Has not the government of Great-Britain been as mild and equitable in the colonies as in any part of her extensive dominions? Has not she been a nursing mother to us from the days of our infancy to this time? Has she not been indulgent almost to a fault? Might not each one of us at this day have sat quietly under his own vine and fig tree, and there have been none to make us afraid, were it not for our own folly? Will not posterity be amazed, when they are told that the present distraction took its rise from a three penny duty on tea, and call it a more unaccountable frenzy, and more disgraceful to the annals of America than that of the witch-craft? . . .

* * *

From what source has the wealth of the colonies flowed? Whence is it derived? Not from agriculture only: Exclusive of commerce the colonies would this day have been a poor people, possessed of little more than the necessaries for supporting life; of course their numbers would be few; for population always keeps pace with the ability of maintaining a family; there would have been but little or no resort of strangers here; the arts and sciences would have made but small progress; the inhabitants would rather have degenerated into a state of ignorance and barbarity. Or had Great-Britain laid such restrictions upon our trade, as our patriots would induce us to believe, that is, had we been pouring the fruits of all our labour into the lap of our parent and been enriching her by the sweat of our brow, without receiving an equivalent, the patrimony derived from our ancestors must have dwindled from little to less, until their posterity should have suffered a general bankruptcy.

But how different are the effects of our connection with, and subordination to Britain! They are too strongly marked to escape the most careless observer: Our merchants are opulent,

and our yeomanry in easier circumstances than the noblesse
of some states: Population is so rapid as to double the number
of inhabitants in the short period of twenty-five years: Cities
are springing up in the depth of the wilderness: Schools, col-
leges, and even universities are interspersed through the continent: Our country abounds with foreign refinements, and
flows with exotic luxuries. These are infallible marks not only
of opulence but of freedom. The recluse may speculate —
the envious repine — the disaffected calumniate — all these
may combine to excite fears and jealousies in the minds of the
multitude, and keep them in alarm from the beginning to the
end of the year; but such evidence as this must forever carry
conviction with it to the minds of the dispassionate and judicious.

Where are the traces of the slavery that our patriots would
terrify us with? The effects of slavery are as glaring and
obvious in those countries that are cursed with its abode, as
the effects of war, pestilence or famine. Our land is not dis-
graced by the wooden shoes of France, or the uncombed hair
of Poland: We have neither racks nor inquisitions, tortures nor
assassinations: The mildness of our criminal jurisprudence is
proverbial, *"a man must have many friends to get hanged in
New England"*. Who has been arbitrarily imprisoned, dis-
seized of his freehold, or dispoiled of his goods? Each peasant
that is industrious may acquire an estate, enjoy it his life time,
and at his death transmit a fair inheritance to his posterity.
The protestant religion is established as far as human laws can
establish it. My dear friends, let me ask each one whether he
has not enjoyed every blessing that is in the power of civil
government to bestow? And yet the parliament has from the
earliest days of the colonies claimed the lately controverted
right both of legislation and taxation, and for more than a
century has been in the actual exercise of it. There is no
grievous exercise of that right at this day, unless the measures
taken to prevent our revolting may be called grievances: Are
we then to rebel lest there should be grievances? Are we to

take up arms and make war against our parent, lest that parent, contrary to the experience of a century and a half, contrary to her own genius, inclination, affection and interest, should treat us or our posterity as bastards and not as sons, and instead of protecting should *enslave* us? The annals of the world have not yet been deformed with a single instance of so unnatural, so causeless, so wanton, so wicked a rebellion. . . .

*   *   *

A congress or convention of committees from the several colonies constitutionally appointed by the supreme authority of the state, or by the several provincial legislatures, amenable to and controlable by the power that convened them, would be salutary in many supposable cases: Such was the convention of 1754; but a congress otherwise appointed, must be an unlawful assembly, wholly incompatible with the constitution, and dangerous in the extreme, more especially as such assemblies wherever chiefly consist of the most violent partizans. The Prince or Sovereign, as some writers call the supreme authority of a state, is sufficiently ample and extensive to provide a remedy for every wrong in all possible emergencies and contingencies; consequently a power that is not derived from such authority, springing up in a state, must incroach upon it, and in proportion as the usurpation inlarges itself, the rightful Prince must be diminished; indeed they cannot long subsist together but must continually militate till one or the other be destroyed. Had the continental congress consisted of committees from the several houses of assembly, although destitute of the consent of the several governors, they would have had some appearance of authority; but many of them were appointed by other committees, as illegally constituted as themselves. However, at so critical and delicate a juncture, Great-Britain being alarmed with an apprehension that the colonies were aiming at independence on the one hand, and the colonies apprehensive of grievous impositions and exactions from Great-Britain, on the other; many real patriots imagined that a congress might be eminently serviceable, that they might prevail on the Bostonians to make restitution to the East-India Company, might still the commotions in this province, remove any ill-founded apprehensions respecting the colonies, and propose some plan for a cordial and permanent reconciliation, which might be adopted by the several assemblies, and make its way through them to the supreme legislature. Placed in this point of light, many good men viewed it with an indulgent eye, and tories as well as whigs, bad the delegates God speed.

The path of duty was too plain to be overlooked, but unfortunately some of the most influential of the members were the very persons that had been the *wilful* cause of the evils they were expected to remedy. Fishing in troubled waters had long been their business and delight, and they deprecated nothing more than that the storm they had blown up, should subside. They were old in intrigue, and would have figured in a conclave. The subtilty, hypocrisy, cunning and chicanery, habitual to such men, were practiced with as much success in this as they had been before in other popular assemblies.

Some of the members, of the first rate abilities, and characters endeavoured to confine the deliberations and resolves of the congress to the design of its institution, which was "to restore peace, harmony and mutual confidence," but were obliged to succumb to the intemperate zeal of some, and at length were so circumvented and wrought upon by the artifice and duplicity of others, as to "lend the sanction of their names to such measures as they condemned in their hearts." Vide a pamphlet published by one of the delegates entitled, A candid examination, &c.

The Congress could not be ignorant of what everybody else knew, that their appointment was repugnant to, and inconsistent with, every idea of government, and therefore wisely determined to destroy it. Their first essay that transpired, and which was matter of no less grief to the friends of our country than of triumph to its enemies was the ever memorable resolve approbating and adopting the Suffolk resolves, thereby undertaking to give a continental sanction to a forcible opposition to acts of parliament, shutting up the courts of justice, and thereby abrogating all human laws, seizing the King's provincial revenue, raising forces in opposition to the King's, and all the tumultuary violence with which this unhappy province has been rent asunder.

This fixed the complexion and marked the character of the congress. We were therefore but little surprized when it was announced, that as far as was in their power, they had dismembered the colonies from the parent country. This they did by resolving that "the colonists are entitled to an exclusive power of legislation in their several provincial legislatures." This stands in its full force, and is an absolute denial of the authority of parliament respecting the colonies. . . .

*   *   *

This is treating Great-Britain as an alien enemy, and if Great-Britain be such, it is justifiable by the law of nations; But their attempt to alienate the affections of the inhabitants of the new conquered province of Quebec from his Majesty's government, is altogether unjustifiable, even upon that principle. In the truly jesuitical address to the Canadians, the congress endeavoured to seduce them from their allegiance, and prevail on them to join the confederacy. After insinuating that they had been tricked, duped, oppressed and enslaved by the Quebec bill, the congress exclaim, why this degrading distinction? "Have not Canadians sense enough to attend to any other publc affairs than gathering stones from one place and piling them up in another? Unhappy people! who are not only injured but *insulted*." "Such a treacherous ingenuity has been exerted in drawing up the code lately offered you, that every sentence beginning with a benevolent pretention, concludes with a destructive power; and the substance of the whole divested of its smooth words, is that the *crown* and its ministers shall be as absolute throughout your extended province as the *despots of Asia or Africa*. We defy you, casting your view upon every side, to discover a single circumstance promising from any quarter, the faintest hope of liberty to you or your posterity, but from an entire adoption to the union of these colonies." The treachery of the congress in this address is the more flagrant, by the Quebec bill's having been adapted to the genius and manners of the Canadians, formed upon their own petition, and received with every testimonial of gratitude. The public tranquility has been often disturbed by treasonable plots and conspiracies. Great-Britain has been repeatedly deluged by the blood of its slaughtered citizens, and shaken to its center by rebellion. — To offer such aggravated insult to British government was a reserve for the *grand continental congress*. None but ideots or madmen, could suppose such measures had a tendency to restore "union and harmony between Great-Britain and the colonies:" Nay! The very demands of the congress evince, that that was not in their intention. — Instead of confining themselves to those acts, which occasioned the misunderstanding, they demand a repeal of fourteen, and bind the colonies by a law not to trade with Great-Britain until that shall be done: Then and not before, the colonists are to treat Great-Britain as an alien friend, and in no other light is the parent country ever after to be viewed; for the parliament is to surcease enacting laws with respect to us for ever. These demands are such as cannot be complied with, consistent with either the honour or interests of the empire, and are therefore insuperable obstacles to a union via congress.

The delegates electing themselves into the States-General or supreme legislature of all the colonies, from *Nova Scotia* to *Georgia*, does not leave a doubt respecting their aiming, in good earnest, at independency: This they did by enacting laws.

WILLIAM EDDIS
*Letters from America, historical and descriptive; comprising oc-
curences from 1769, to 1777, inclusive.*

London, 1792, pp. 189–201

Annapolis, March 13th, 1775

There is but too much reason to apprehend that the hour
is approaching when even the intercourse of letters will
be greatly interrupted, if not totally prohibited.

From one extremity of this continent to the other,
every appearance indicates approaching hostilities. The
busy voice of preparation echoes through every settlement; and those who are not zealously infected with the
general frenzy, are considered as enemies to the cause of
liberty; and, without regard to any peculiarity of situation, are branded with opprobrious appellations, and
pointed out as victims to public resentment.

Very considerable subscriptions have been made in
every quarter, for the relief of the Bostonians: large
sums have likewise been collected for the purchase of
arms and ammunition, and persons of all denominations
are required to associate under military regulations, on
pain of the severest censure; every measure, while tending to the most fatal consequences, is eagerly and wildly
pursued.

Admitting the evils complained of to be founded on
reality, the mode adopted to obtain redress cannot, in
my opinion, be justified on principles of reason or sound
policy. I have, therefore, refused to join in any of the
proposed contributions; to appear in any of their associations; or to enrol in any military corps. I have even
attempted to moderate the enthusiasm of intemperate

zeal, by the following appeal to Common Sense and Common Equity; which, through the medium of the Maryland Gazette, has been submitted to public inspection; and if favourable conclusions may be drawn from appearances, it has been received with considerable approbation, my letter having already been reprinted in almost every paper throughout this continent.

TO THE PRINTERS

The present unhappy contention between the *mother country* and her *colonies*, is a matter of the deepest concern to every honest, every feeling mind: it is, therefore, the indispensable duty of every friend to society, to study and to pursue those methods, which may lead to a perfect reconciliation, and the establishment of a permanent union between *Great Britain* and *America*.

The principle of *parliamentary taxation* over this extensive part of the empire, is generally denied by all ranks, and denominations of men; the grand subject of controversy, therefore, that prevails at present, respects *the most eligible method to obtain redress*. On this point, there appears a division of sentiment, which has given rise to *heart-burnings and discontent;* and, in some degree, struck at the root of that harmony which, at this important period, ought to *guide* and *influence* every action.

In opposition to measures dictated by *calmness* and *moderation*, (a steady adherence to which, it was generally supposed, would be attended with the most happy effects) *a military appearance* is assumed — *subscriptions* are industriously making for the purchase of *arms, ammunition,* &c. and the *severest censure* is indiscriminately passed on those persons who happen to dissent from the popular opinion, and prefer more conciliating methods of accommodation.

It is certain that there are many in *this,* and other *provinces,* who object to the spirit of violence, which seems at this time too predominant. Convinced of the propriety of their sentiments, and in the integrity of their hearts, they conceive the cause of America may be *totally injured* by a precipitate, and unnecessary defiance of the power of

Great Britain: they firmly believe, that a respectful behaviour to their *sovereign* and their *mother country* — a
dutiful and constitutional application to the *throne* — and
a firm perseverance in *virtuous*, though *pacific principles*,
will, in the issue, be productive of the most felicitous consequences. Actuated by such considerations, they cannot
be reconciled to those violent extremes which have been
too rashly adopted by many; and which they are anxious
to establish, as the *only* feasible plan of terminating the
present dissensions.

On deliberate reflection, it can hardly be imagined, that
the mother country has formed the least intention of reducing these provinces to a state of abject servility, by the
force of arms; the *natural connexion* — the *close ties* — and
nice dependencies, which exist between the different parts
of the empire, forbid indulging any conclusions of so melancholy a nature. She will be more just — more tender to
her offspring — the voice of reason will prevail — our
grievances will be redressed — and she will be found, *to
the end of time*, a kind — a fostering parent! — But admitting that Great Britain were determined to enforce a submission to all her mandates; even in that case, we have
little cause to apprehend, that she will *unsheath the
sword*, and establish her decrees in *the blood of thousands*.
A more safe and certain method is obvious: a small proportion of *her naval power* would entirely shut up our
harbours — suspend our trade — impoverish the inhabitants
— promote intestine divisions — and involve us in all the
horrors of anarchy and confusion. To avoid evils, *even
great as these*, we are not meanly to bend the neck, and
submit to every innovation. But when there is no prospect of such dreadful calamities, why are we to form
ideas of *battles* and of *slaughter?* Why are our coasts to
resound with *hostile preparations?* — the demon of *discord*
to stalk at large — and *friends* and *kindred* forget the
peaceful bonds of *amity* and *love?*

It has been objected by the advocates for moderation,
that the methods pursued to complete the subscription for
arms, &c. has more the complexion of *an arbitrary tax*,
than *a voluntary contribution.* On the other hand, it has
been asserted, "that money raised in a manner, where there
is no obligation to pay but a sense of duty; and no other
mode to induce compliance, but shame and infamy, cannot

be deemed *a tax*." A sense of duty is, undoubtedly, the
most noble incentive to *worthy actions;* but a false dread
of *shame* and *infamy*, has perverted many *an honest heart*,
and too frequently proved an irresistible temptation to
dishonourable practices. Let us a moment reflect: — Can
there be an imposition more arbitrary and severe, than a
necessity of assenting to any particular measure, or for-
feiting *that fair* — that *unsullied reputation*, which allevi-
ates the cares of life, and smooths the inevitable rugged
path to the dreary mansions of the grave!

> Good name in man and woman
> Is the immediate jewel of their souls.
> Who steals my purse, steals trash; 'tis something,
>   nothing;
> 'Twas mine, 'tis his, and has been slave to thousands;
> But he that filches from me my good name,
> Robs me of that which not enriches him,
> And makes me poor indeed. —

If I differ in opinion from the multitude, must I therefore be deprived of my character, and the confidence of
my fellow-citizens, when in every station of life I discharge my duty with fidelity and honour? DEATH — the
certain tax on all the sons of men, were preferable to so
abject a state. — No — 'twere better to suffer all that "age,
ach, penury, imprisonment, can lay on nature," than resign that glorious inheritance of a free subject — the liberty
of *thinking — speaking —* and *acting*, agreeable to the dictates of conscience! I frankly acknowledge no man has a
right to disturb the peace of the community, by broach-
ing tenets destructive to the *true interests* and *welfare* of
his country; but at the same time, it cannot be justifiable
to compel others to adopt *every system* which we esteem conducive to the public good. Let us therefore be
unanimous in *virtue* — in *frugality* — and in *industry;* let
us conduct ourselves on the christian principle of "doing
to others as we would have done to us;" let us not, in the
frantic moments of intemperate zeal, mistake *libertinism*
for *liberty*, and commit outrages, which we shall recollect
with *shame*, and condemn with *heart-felt anxiety.* While
we contend for the inestimable blessings of British subjects, let us not assume a *tyrannical authority* over each
other. In a word, let *reason* and *moderation* hold the scale

in every important determination — so shall every *real grievance* be effectually redressed — every man shall sing the song of gladness under his own *vine*, and we shall at once be free — be loyal — and be happy!

I am, Sir,

Most sincerely,

Annapolis,
Feb. 14, 1775

A Friend to Amity.

On perusing the above humble effort of my pen, it will readily occur to you, that if I had, in the most distant manner, admitted the right of parliamentary taxation, my address, in times like these, could not possibly have been productive of any salutary consequences. The denial of that right being the prevailing creed of the colonies, I found myself necessitated to coincide with the popular opinion, that I might strike, with the greater efficacy, at that vindictive, arbitrary system, which under the fallacious pretence of supporting the interests of constitutional freedom, exerts a tyrannical authority, in order to enforce hostile opposition in preference to moderate and respectful applications.

How far the legislative authority of Great Britain legally extends over the American Provinces, is beyond the extent of my limited abilities to determine. In the confidence of conversation, I daily hear various opinions, supported by strength of argument and accuracy of observation, and from what I have heard, and am enabled to judge, I am clearly convinced that much more is apprehended than has any existence in reality. But in all countries there are busy, turbulent spirits, who from motives of ambition, avarice, or discontent, "infect the general ear with horrid speech:" by eagerly pressing forwards, as champions in the public cause, they agitate the passions of the misguided multitude, and imperceptibly lead them to the most dreadful extremities.

It is with pleasure I am able to assert, that a greater degree of moderation appears to predominate in this province, than in any other on the continent; and I am perfectly assured we are very materially indebted for this peculiar advantage to the collected and consistent conduct of our Governor, whose views appear solely directed to advance the interests of the community; and to preserve, by every possible method, the public tranquillity. How long we may continue thus distinguished, time alone must determine. Should our demagogues obtain the ascendency, after which they labour, we shall assuredly equal any of our neighbours in those violences of which we now only contemplate the commencement.

While the power of communicating my sentiments, *with safety*, is happily continued, I shall not fail to give you due information of every material circumstance.

PART TWO

CHAPTER 4

Common Sense Versus True Interest

By January 1776, the Anglo-American quarrel had gone beyond argument and now entered the phase of denunciation. It was no longer necessary to justify colonial grievances, but to inspire men to action. Thomas Paine (1737–1809), born at Thetford, England, had pursued a variety of unsuccessful vocations before coming to America in 1774 with Franklin's commendation. Within two years of his arrival, Paine published *Common Sense*, one of the most effective polemics ever written. He was able to destroy the last sentimental links between Britain and the colonies with a thoroughness no native born American had dared attempt. After his work, it was impossible to maintain the distinction between George III and his ministry that had been made by so many incipient revolutionaries. Henceforth George received all the blame, and colonial sentiment began to find a new focus for loyalty: America.

To many, however, the violent response of a Tom Paine far exceeded the provocation from Britain. There were several rebuttals to his pamphlet which, while they lacked the impact of *Common Sense*, still represented a large body of American opinion. Such opposing views were expressed by Charles Inglis (1734–1816), himself a pamphleteer of no mean ability. An Episcopalian minister, curate and later rector of Trinity

Church, New York City, Inglis had engaged in the literary
warfare of the 1760's over the proposed introduction of bish-
ops to America. In 1776 he took up his pen to argue that a
break with the mother country was not merely unjustified
but unnatural, and an attempt to gain independence would be
fraught with as many dangers in success as in failure. There
was still time, he hoped, for men of good will to reconcile the
two sides. Banished by the revolutionaries, Inglis became
Bishop of Nova Scotia after the war, and devoted his remaining years to preventing the reappearance, in his new province,
of those character defects that once had led so many colonials
to rebellion.

THOMAS   PAINE

Common Sense, *in The Political Writings of Thomas Paine, 2 vols.
Boston, 1859, Vol. I, pp. 34–39, 41–43*

. . . As much hath been said of the advantages of reconciliation, which, like an agreeable dream, hath passed away and
left us as we were, it is but right that we should examine the
contrary side of the argument, and inquire into some of the
many material injuries which these colonies sustain, and always
will sustain, by being connected with and dependent on Great
Britain. To examine that connexion and dependence, on the
principles of nature and common sense, to see what we
have to trust to, if separated, and what we are to expect, if
dependent.

I have heard it asserted by some, that as America has flourished under her former connexion with Great Britain, that
same connexion is necessary towards her future happiness, and
will always have the same effect. Nothing can be more
fallacious than this kind of argument. We may as well assert
that because a child has thrived upon milk, that it is never to
have meat, or that the first twenty years of our lives is to

become a precedent for the next twenty. But even this is admitting more than is true, for I answer roundly, that America would have flourished as much, and probably much more, had no European power had any thing to do with her. The articles of commerce, by which she has enriched herself, are the necessaries of life, and will always have a market while eating is the custom of Europe.

But she has protected us, say some. That she hath engrossed us is true, and defended the continent at our expense as well as her own, is admitted, and she would have defended Turkey from the same motives, *viz.* for the sake of trade and dominion.

Alas! We have been long led away by ancient prejudices, and made large sacrifices to superstition. We have boasted the protection of Great Britain, without considering, that her motive was *interest* not *attachment;* and that she did not protect us from our enemies on *our account*, but from *her enemies on her own account*, from those who had no quarrel with us on any *other account*, and who will always be our enemies on the *same account*. Let Britain waive her pretensions to the continent, or the continent throw off the dependence, and we should be at peace with France and Spain, were they at war with Britain. The miseries of Hanover last war ought to warn us against connexions. . . .

* * *

But Britain is the parent country, say some. Then the more shame upon her conduct. Even brutes do not devour their young, nor savages make war upon their families; wherefore the assertion, if true, turns to her reproach; but it happens not to be true, or only partly so, and the phrase *parent* or *mother country* hath been jesuitically adopted by the king and his parasites, with a low papistical design of gaining an unfair bias on the credulous weakness of our minds. Europe, and not England, is the parent country of America. This new world hath been the asylum for the persecuted lovers of civil and religious liberty from *every part* of Europe. Hither have they fled, not from the tender embraces of the mother, but from the cruelty of the monster; and it is so far true of England, that the same tyranny which drove the first emigrants from home, pursues their descendants still. . . .

* * *

Much hath been said of the united strength of Britain and the colonies, that in conjunction they might bid defiance to the world. But this is mere presumption; the fate of war is uncertain, neither do the expressions mean any thing; for this continent would never suffer itself to be drained of inhabitants, to support the British arms in either Asia, Africa, or Europe.

Besides, what have we to do with setting the world at defiance? Our plan is commerce, and that, well attended to, will secure us the peace and friendship of all Europe; because it is the interest of all Europe to have America a *free port*. Her trade will always be a protection, and her barrenness of gold and silver secure her from invaders.

I challenge the warmest advocate for reconciliation, to show a single advantage that this continent can reap, by being connected with Great Britain. I repeat the challenge; not a single advantage is derived. Our corn will fetch its price in any market in Europe and our imported goods must be paid for, buy them where we will.

But the injuries and disadvantages which we sustain by that connexion, are without number; and our duty to mankind at large, as well as to ourselves, instructs us to renounce the alliance; because, any submission to or dependence on Great Britain, tends directly to involve this continent in European wars and quarrels; and sets us at variance with nations, who would otherwise seek our friendship, and against whom, we have neither anger nor complaint. As Europe is our market for trade, we ought to form no partial connexion with any part of it. It is the true interest of America to steer clear of European contentions, which she never can do, while, by her dependence on Britain, she is made the make-weight in the scale of British politics.

Europe is too thickly planted with kingdoms to be long at peace, and whenever a war breaks out between England and any foreign power, the trade of America goes to ruin, *because of her connexion with Britain.* The next war may not turn out like the last, and should it not, the advocates for reconciliation now will be wishing for separation then, because, neutrality in that case, would be a safer convoy than a man of war. Everything that is right or natural pleads for separation. The blood of the slain, the weeping voice of nature cries, *'tis time to part.* Even the distance at which the Almighty hath placed England and America, is a strong and natural proof, that the authority of the one over the other, was never the design of heaven. The time likewise at which the continent was discovered, adds weight to the argument, and the manner in which it was peopled, increases the force of it. The reformation was preceded by the discovery of America, as if the Almighty graciously meant to open a sanctuary to the persecuted in future years, when home should afford neither friendship nor safety.

The authority of Great Britain over this continent, is a form of government, which sooner or later must have an end: and a serious mind can draw no true pleasure by looking forward, under the painful and positive conviction, that what he calls "the present constitution," is merely temporary. As parents, we can have no joy, knowing that *this government* is not sufficiently lasting to ensure any thing which we may bequeath to posterity: and by a plain method of argument, as we are running the next generation into debt, we ought to do the work of it, otherwise we use them meanly and pitifully. In order to discover the line of our duty rightly, we should take our children in our hand, and fix our station a few years farther into life; that eminence will present a prospect, which a few present fears and prejudices conceal from our sight.

Though I would carefully avoid giving unnecessary offence, yet I am inclined to believe, that all those who espouse the doctrine of reconciliation, may be included within the following descriptions.

Interested men who are not to be trusted; weak men, who cannot see; prejudiced men, who will not see; and a certain set of moderate men, who think better of the European world than it deserves: and this last class, by an ill-judged deliberation, will be the cause of more calamities to this continent than all the other three. . . .

*　　*　　*

Men of passive tempers look somewhat lightly over the offences of Britain, and, still hoping for the best, are apt to call out, *"come, come, we shall be friends again for all this."* But examine the passions and feelings of mankind, bring the doctrine of reconciliation to the touchstone of nature, and then tell me, whether you can hereafter love, honor, and faithfully serve the power that hath carried fire and sword into your land. If you cannot do all these, then you are only deceiving yourselves, and by your delay bringing ruin upon your posterity. Your future connexion with Britain, whom you can neither love nor honor, will be forced and unnatural, and being formed only on the plan of present convenience, will in a little time fall into a relapse more wretched than the first. But if you say, you can still pass the violations over, then I ask, hath your house been burnt? Hath your property been destroyed before your face? Are your wife and children destitute of a bed to lie on, or bread to live on? Have you lost a parent or a child by their hands, and yourself the ruined and wretched survivor? If you have not, then are you not a judge of those who have. But if you have, and can still shake hands with the murderers, then are you unworthy the name of husband, father, friend, or lover, and whatever may be your rank or title in life, you have the heart of a coward, and the spirit of a sycophant.

This is not inflaming or exaggerating matters, but trying them by those feelings and affections which nature justifies, and without which, we should be incapable of discharging the social duties of life, or enjoying the felicities of it. I mean not to exhibit horror for the purpose of provoking revenge, but to awaken us from fatal and unmanly slumbers, that we may pursue determinately some fixed object. It is not in the power of Britain or of Europe to conquer America, if she does not conquer herself by delay and timidity. The present winter is worth an age if rightly employed, but if lost or neglected, the whole continent will partake of the misfortune: and there is no punishment which that man will not deserve, be he who, or what, or where he will, that may be the means of sacrificing a season so precious and useful.

It is repugnant to reason, and the universal order of things, to all examples from former ages, to suppose that this continent can longer remain subject to any external power. The most sanguine in Britain, do not think so. The utmost stretch of human wisdom cannot, at this time, compass a plan short of separation, which can promise the continent even a year's security. Reconciliation is *now* a fallacious dream. Nature hath deserted the connexion, and art cannot supply her place. For, as Milton wisely expresses, "never can true reconcilement grow, where wounds of deadly hate have pierced so deep." . . .

* * *

But admitting that matters were now made up, what would be the event? I answer, the ruin of the continent. And that for several reasons.

1st, The powers of governing still remaining in the hands of the king, he will have a negative over the whole legislation of this continent. And as he hath shown himself such an inveterate enemy to liberty, and discovered such a thirst for arbitrary power: is he, or is he not, a proper person to say to these colonies, "*You shall make no laws but what I please!*" And is

there any inhabitant of America so ignorant as not to know,
that according to what is called the *present constitution*, this
continent can make no laws but what the king gives leave to?
and is there any man so unwise as not to see, that (considering
what has happened) he will suffer no law to be made here, but
such as suits *his* purpose? We may be as effectually enslaved
by the want of laws in America, as by submitting to laws made
for us in England. After matters are made up (as it is called)
can there be any doubt, but the whole power of the crown
will be exerted, to keep this continent as low and humble as
possible? Instead of going forward we shall go backward, or
be perpetually quarrelling, or ridiculously petitioning. — We
are already greater than the king wishes us to be, and will he
not hereafter endeavor to make us less? To bring the matter
to one point, Is the power who is jealous of our prosperity, a
proper power to govern us? Whoever says *No*, to this question, is an *independent*, for independency means no more than
this, whether we shall make our own laws, or, whether the
king, the greatest enemy which this continent hath, or can
have, shall tell us "*there shall be no laws but such as I like.*"

But the king, you will say, has a negative in England; the
people there can make no laws without his consent. In point
of right and good order, it is something very ridiculous, that
a youth of twenty-one (which hath often happened) shall say
to several millions of people, older and wiser than himself, I
forbid this or that act of yours to be law. But in this case I
decline this sort of reply, though I will never cease to expose
the absurdity of it; and only answer, that England being the
King's residence, and America not, makes quite another case.
The king's negative *here* is ten times more dangerous and
fatal than it can be in England; for *there* he will scarcely refuse
his consent to a bill for putting England into as strong a state
of defence as possible, and in America he would never suffer
such a bill to be passed.

America is only a secondary object in this system of British
politics — England consults the good of *this* country no fur-

ther than it answers her *own* purpose. Wherefore, her own interest leads to suppress the growth of *ours* in every case which doth not promote her advantage, or in the least interferes with it. A pretty state we should soon be in under such a second-hand government, considering what has happened! Men do not change from enemies to friends, by the alteration of a name: and in order to show that reconciliation now is a dangerous doctrine, I affirm, *that it would be policy in the king at this time, to repeal the acts, for the sake of reinstating himself in the government of the provinces; in order that he may accomplish by craft and subtlety, in the long run, what he cannot do by force in the short one.* Reconciliation and ruin are nearly related.

2dly, That as even the best terms, which we can expect to obtain, can amount to no more than a temporary expedient, or a kind of government by guardianship, which can last no longer than till the colonies come of age, so the general face and state of things, in the interim, will be unsettled and unpromising. Emigrants of property will not choose to come to a country whose form of government hangs but by a thread, and which is every day tottering on the brink of commotion and disturbance; and numbers of the present inhabitants would lay hold of the interval, to dispose of their effects, and quit the continent.

But the most powerful of all arguments, is, that nothing but independence, i.e. a continental form of government, can keep the peace of the continent and preserve it inviolate from civil wars. I dread the event of a reconciliation with Britain now, as it is more than probable that it will be followed by a revolt somewhere or other, the consequences of which may be far more fatal than all the malice of Britain.

Thousands are already ruined by British barbarity. (Thousands more will probably suffer the same fate.) Those men have other feelings than us who have suffered nothing. All they *now* possess is liberty, what they before enjoyed is sacrificed to its service, and having nothing more to lose, they disdain submission. Besides, the general temper of the colonies, towards a British government, will be like that of a youth, who is nearly out of his time; they will care very little about her. And a government which cannot preserve the peace, is no government at all, and in that case we pay our money for nothing; and pray what is it that Britain can do, whose power will be wholly on paper, should a civil tumult break out the very day after reconciliation? I have heard some men say, many of whom I believe spoke without thinking, that they dreaded an independence, fearing that it would produce civil wars. It is but seldom that our first thoughts are truly correct, and that is the case here, for there is ten times more to dread from a patched up connexion than from independence. . . .

*   *   *

However, it matters very little now, what the king of England either says or does; he hath wickedly broken through every moral and human obligation, trampled nature and conscience beneath his feet; and by a steady and constitutional spirit of insolence and cruelty, procured for himself an universal hatred. It is *now* the interest of America to provide for herself. She hath already a large and young family, whom it is more her duty to take care of, than to be granting away her property to support a power which is become a reproach to the names of men and Christians — *Ye,* whose office it is to watch over the morals of a nation, of whatsoever sect or denomination ye are of, as well as ye who are more immediately the guardians of the public liberty, if you wish to preserve your native country uncontaminated by European corruption, ye must in secret wish a separation — but leaving the moral part to private reflection, I shall chiefly confine my further remarks to the following heads:

1st, That it is the interest of America to be separated from Britain.

2d, Which is the easiest and most practicable plan, *reconciliation* or *independence?* with some occasional remarks.

In support of the first, I could, if I judged it proper, produce the opinion of some of the ablest and most experienced men on this continent: and whose sentiments on that head, are not yet publicly known. It is in reality a self-evident position: for no nation in a state of foreign dependance, limited in its commerce, and cramped and fettered in its legislative powers, can ever arrive at any material eminence. America doth not yet know what opulence is; and although the progress which she hath made stands unparalleled in the history of other nations, it is but childhood, compared with what she would be capable of arriving at, had she, as she ought to have, the legislative powers in her own hands. England is, at this time, proudly coveting what would do her no good were she to accomplish it; and the continent hesitating on a matter which will be her final ruin if neglected. It is the commerce and not the conquest of America by which England is to be benefited, and that would in a great measure continue, were the countries as independent of each other as France and Spain; because in many articles neither can go to a better market. But it is the independence of this country of Britain, or any other, which is now the main and only object worthy of contention, and which, like all other truths discovered by necessity, will appear clearer and stronger every day.

1st, Because it will come to that one time or other.

2d, Because the longer it is delayed, the harder it will be to accomplish.

I have frequently amused myself both in public and private companies, with silently remarking the specious errors of those who speak without reflecting. And among the many which I have heard, the following seems the most general, *viz.* that if this rupture should happen forty or fifty years hence, instead

of now, the continent would be more able to shake off the
dependance. To which I reply, that our military ability, *at
this time*, arises from the experience gained in the last war, and
which in forty or fifty years time, would be totally extinct.
The continent would not, by that time, have a general, or
even a military officer left; and we, or those who may succeed
us, would be as ignorant of martial matters as the ancient
Indians: and this single position, closely attended to, will
unanswerably prove that the present time is preferable to all
others. The argument turns thus — at the conclusion of the
last war, we had experience, but wanted numbers; and forty
or fifty years hence, we shall have numbers, without experience; wherefore the proper point of time, must be some particular point between the two extremes, in which a sufficiency
of the former remains, and a proper increase of the latter
is obtained: and that point of time is the present time.

The reader will pardon this digression, as it does not properly come under the head I first set out with, and to which
I again return by the following position, *viz.*

Should affairs be patched up with Britain, and she remain
the governing and sovereign power of America, (which,
as matters are now circumstanced, is giving up the point
entirely) we shall deprive ourselves of the very means of
sinking the debt we have, or may contract. The value of
the back lands, which some of the provinces are clandestinely
deprived of, by the unjust extension of the limits of Canada,
valued only at five pounds sterling per hundred acres, amount
to upwards of twenty-five millions Pennsylvania currency;
and the quit-rents at one penny sterling per acre, to two
millions yearly.

It is by the sale of those lands that the debt may be sunk,
without burden to any, and the quit-rent reserved thereon,
will always lessen, and in time, will wholly support the yearly
expense of government. It matters not how long the debt
is in paying, so that the lands when sold be applied to the

discharge of it, and for the execution of which, the congress for the time being, will be the continental trustees.

I proceed now to the second head, *viz.* Which is the easiest and most practicable plan, *reconciliation* or *independence?* with some occasional remarks.

He who takes nature for his guide, is not easily beaten out of his argument, and on that ground, I answer generally — *That* INDEPENDENCE *being a* SINGLE SIMPLE LINE, *contained within ourselves, and reconciliation, a matter exceedingly perplexed and complicated, and in which a treacherous, capricious court is to interfere, gives the answer without a doubt.*

The present state of America is truly alarming to every man who is capable of reflection. Without law, without government, without any other mode of power or what is founded on, and granted by, courtesy. Held together by an unexampled occurrence of sentiment, which is nevertheless subject to change, and which every secret enemy is endeavouring to dissolve. Our present condition is, legislation without law; wisdom without a plan; a constitution without a name; and what is strangely astonishing, perfect independence contending for dependence. The instance is without a precedent; the case never existed before; and, who can tell what may be the event? The property of no man is secure in the present unbraced system of things. The mind of the multitude is left at random, and seeing no fixed object before them, they pursue such as fancy or opinion presents. Nothing is criminal; there is no such thing as treason; wherefore, every one thinks himself at liberty to act as he pleases. The tories dared not have assembled offensively, had they known that their lives by that act, were forfeited to the laws of the state. A line of distinction should be drawn between English soldiers taken in battle, and inhabitants of America taken in arms. The first are prisoners, but the latter traitors. The one forfeits his liberty, the other his head.

CHARLES   INGLIS
An American, The True Interest of America Impartially Stated.
Philadelphia, Humphries, 1776
pp. 10, 40, 47–53, 67–68, 70–71

The author of a pamphlet, falsely and absurdly entitled COMMON SENSE, is . . . chargeable with a . . . design of rending the British Empire asunder. To realize his beloved scheme of Independent Republicanism, he would persuade the colonists to renounce their allegiance to our true and lawful liege sovereign King GEORGE III — plunge themselves into a tedious, bloody, and most expensive war with Great Britain — and risque their lives, liberties and property on the dubious event of that war.

This is the principal object his pamphlet has in view; other things are only mentioned as conducive to that end. To prepare the reader for it — to take off that horror which every honest man and well-informed friend of America must naturally feel at a proposal so wicked and ruinous; he first treats some of the matters which he fashions to his purpose. He poisons the fountain that the stream may be rejected. . . . He pathetically laments, that — "Alas! We have been long led away by ancient prejudices, and made large sacrifices to superstition — not considering that the motive of Great-Britain in protecting us, was interest, not attachment;" and then he spins out a tedious, affected sentence of her "not protecting us from our enemies on our account, but from her enemies on her own account," &c. Supposing this were true, where is the harm? Great-Britain actually *did* protect us; and it is a matter of little moment to us, what her motives were. If she received benefit by it, so much the better. Mutual interest is the strongest bond of union between states, as the history of mankind testifies; and certainly that nation would act a most absurd, as well as wicked part, which lavished away its blood and treasure, without any prospect of national advantage in

return. But I firmly believe, that his assertions on this head
are as false, as they are ungenerous; and that Great-Britain,
in protecting us, was actuated by motives of affection and
attachment, as well as interest. The whole of her conduct
to the colonies, till lately, evinces it — the Americans themselves have acknowledged it. Great-Britain, no doubt derived
many advantages from the colonies; but should we undervalue
her protection on that account, or ascribe it to sordid motives
only? It is every man's interest as well as duty to be honest;
would it, therefore, be candid, generous or true, to suppose,
that every honest man is actuated by selfishness only? — But
candour and truth are things that have nothing to do with
the procedure of this dark republican, who aims at utterly
effacing every trace of former affection and friendship between Great-Britain and the colonies; and like a fiend that
delighted in human misery, would arm them with the most
deadly, irreconcileable hatred against each other.

But our author now waxes so exceedingly warm, and assumes
so terrific an air, that I almost dread to approach him. "I
challenge," says he, "the warmest advocate for reconciliation,
to show a single advantage that this country can reap by
being connected with Great-Britain, I repeat the challenge,
not a single advantage is derived." . . .

I think it no very difficult matter to point out many advantages which will certainly attend our reconciliation and connection with Great-Britain, on a firm, constitutional plan. I
shall select a few of these; and that their importance may be
more clearly discerned, I shall afterwards point out some of
the evils which inevitably must attend our separating from
Britain, and declaring for Independency. On each article I
shall study brevity.

1. By a Reconciliation with Britain, a period would be put
to the present calamitous war, by which so many lives have
been lost and so many more will be lost, if it continues. This
alone is an advantage devoutly to be wished for. This author

says — "the blood of the slain, the weeping voice of nature cries. 'Tis time to part." I think they cry just the reverse. The blood of the slain, the weeping voice of nature, cries — It is time to be reconciled, it is time to lay aside those animosities which have pushed on Britons to shed the blood of Britons; it is high time that those who are connected by the enduring ties of religion, kindred and country should resume their former friendship, and be united in the bond of mutual affection, as their interests are inseparably united.

2. By a Reconciliation with Great-Britain — Peace — that fairest offspring and gift of Heaven — will be restored. In one respect Peace is like health; we do not sufficiently know its value but by its absence. What uneasiness and anxiety, what evils has this short interruption of peace with the parent state brought on the whole British Empire! Let every man only consult his feelings — I except my antagonist — and it will require no great force of rhetoric to convince him, that a removal of those evils, and a restoration of peace, would be a singular advantage and blessing.

3. Agriculture, commerce, and industry would resume their wonted vigor. At present they languish and droop, both here and in Britain; and must continue to do so, while this unhappy contest remains unsettled.

4. By a connection with Great-Britain, our trade would still have the protection of the greatest naval power in the world. England has the advantage, in this respect, of every other state, whether of ancient or modern times. Her insular situation, her nursery for seamen, the superiority of those seamen above others — these circumstances to mention no other, combine to make her the first maritime power in the universe — such exactly is the power whose protection we want for our commerce. To suppose with our author, that we should have no war, were we to revolt from England, is too absurd to deserve a confutation. I could just as soon set about refuting the reveries of some brain-sick enthusiast. Past experience shows that Britain is able to defend our commerce, and our coasts;

and we have no reason to doubt of her being able to do so for the future.

5. The protection of our trade, while connected with Britain, will not cost us a *fiftieth* part of what it must cost, were we ourselves to raise a naval force sufficient for the purpose.

6. Whilst connected with Great-Britain, we have a bounty on almost every article of exportation; and we may be better supplied with goods by her, than we could elsewhere. What our author says is true — "That our imported goods must be paid for, buy them where we will;" but we may buy them dearer, and of worse quality, in one place than another. The manufactures of Great-Britain confessedly surpass any in the world — particularly those in every kind of metal which we want most; and no country can afford linens and woollens, of equal quality cheaper.

7. When a Reconciliation is effected, and things return into the old channel, a few years of peace will restore everything to its pristine state. Emigrants will flow in as usual from the different parts of Europe. Population will advance with the same rapid progress as formerly, and our lands will rise in value.

These advantages are not imaginary but real. They are such as we have already experienced; and such as we may derive from a connection with Great-Britain for ages to come. Each of these might easily be enlarged on, and others added to them; but I only mean to suggest a few hints to the reader.

Let us now, if you please, take a view of the other side of the question. Suppose we were to revolt from Great-Britain, declare ourselves independent, and set up a Republic of our own — what would be the consequence? — I stand aghast at the prospect — my blood runs chill when I think of the calamities, the complicated evils that must ensue, and must be clearly foreseen — it is impossible for any man to foresee them all. Our author cautiously avoids saying anything of the inconveniences that would attend a separation. He does not even suppose that

any inconvenience would attend it. Let us only declare ourselves independent, break loose from Great-Britain, and according to him, a Paradisaical state will follow! But a prudent
man will consider and weigh matters well before he consents
to such a measure — when on the brink of such a dreadful
precipice, he must necessarily recoil, and think of the consequences, before he advances a step forward. Supposing then
we declared for Independency — what would follow? — I
answer —

1. All our property throughout the continent would be
unhinged; the greatest confusion, and most violent convulsion
would take place. . . . the old constitution would be totally
subverted. The common bond that tied us together and by
which our property was secured, would be snapt asunder. It
is not to be doubted but our Congress would endeavour to
apply some remedy for those evils; but with all deference to
that respectable body, I do not apprehend that any remedy in
their power would be adequate, at least for some time. I do not
choose to be more explicit; but I am able to support my
opinion.

2. What a horrid situation would thousands be reduced to
who have taken the oath of allegiance to the King; yet contrary
to their oath, as well as to their inclination, must be compelled
to renounce that allegiance, or abandon all their property in
America! How many thousands more would be reduced to a
similar situation; who, although they took not that oath, yet
would think it inconsistent with their duty and a good conscience to renounce their Sovereign; I dare say these will
appear trifling difficulties to our author; but whatever he may
think, there are thousands and thousands who would sooner
lose all they had in the world, nay life itself, than thus wound
their conscience. A Declaration of Independency would infallibly disunite and divide the colonists.

3. By a Declaration for Independency, every avenue to an
accommodation with Great-Britain would be closed; the sword

only could then decide the quarrel; and the sword would not be sheathed till one had conquered the other.

The importance of these colonies to Britain need not be enlarged on, it is a thing so universally known. The greater their importance is to her, so much the more obstinate will her struggle be not to lose them. The independency of America would, in the end, deprive her of the West Indies, shake her empire to the foundation, and reduce her to a state of the most mortifying insignificance. Great Britain therefore must, for her own preservation, risk every thing, and exert her whole strength, to prevent such an event from taking place. This being the case —

4. Devastation and ruin must mark the progress of this war along the sea coast of America. Hitherto, Britain has not exerted her power. . . . But as soon as we declare for independency, every prospect of this kind must vanish. Ruthless war, with all its aggravated horrors, will ravage our once happy land — our sea coasts and ports will be ruined, and our ships taken. Torrents of blood will be spilt, and thousands reduced to beggary and wretchedness.

This melancholy contest would last until one side conquered. Supposing Britain to be victorious, however high my opinion is of British Generosity, I should be exceedingly sorry to receive terms from her in the haughty tone of a conquerer. Or supposing such a failure of her manufactures, commerce and strength, that victory should incline to the side of America; yet who can say in that case, what extremities her sense of resentment and self preservation will drive Great Britain to? For my part, I should not in the least be surprised, if on such a prospect as the independency of America she would parcel out this continent to the different European Powers. Canada might be restored to France, Florida to Spain, with additions to each — other states might also come in for a portion. Let no man think this chimerical or improbable. The independency of America would be so fatal to Britain, that she would leave nothing in her power undone to prevent it. I believe as firmly as I do my own existence, that if every other method failed, she would try some such expedient as this, to disconcert our scheme of independency; and let any man figure to himself the situation of these British colonies, if only Canada were restored to France!

5. But supposing once more that we were able to cut off every regiment that Britain can spare or hire, and to destroy every ship that she can send — that we could beat off any other European power that would presume to intrude upon this continent: Yet, a republican form of government would neither suit the genius of the people, nor the extent of America. . . .

The Americans are properly Britons. They have the manners, habits, and ideas of Britons; and have been accustomed to a similar form of government. But Britons never could bear the extremes, either of monarchy or republicanism. Some of their kings have aimed at despotism; but always failed. Repeated efforts have been made towards democracy, and they equally failed. Once indeed, republicanism triumphed over the constitution; the despotism of one person ensued; both were finally expelled. The inhabitants of Great Britain were quite anxious for the restoration of *royalty* in 1660, as they were for its expulsion in 1642, and for some succeeding years. If we may judge our future events by past transactions, in similar circumstances, this would most probably be the case of America, were a republican form of government adopted in our present ferment. After much blood was shed, those confusions would terminate in the despotism of some one successful adventurer; and should the Americans be so fortunate as to emancipate themselves from that thraldom, perhaps the whole would end in a limited monarchy, after shedding as much more blood. Limited monarchy is the form of government which is most favourable to liberty — which is best adapted to the genius and temper of Britons; although here and there among us a crack-brained zealot for democracy or absolute monarchy, may be sometimes found.

Besides the unsuitableness of the republican form to the genius of the people, America is too extensive for it. That form may do well enough for a single city, or small territory; but would be utterly improper for such a continent as this. America is too unwieldy for the feeble, dilatory administration of democracy. . . .

6. In fine. Let us, for a moment, imagine that an American republic is formed, every obstacle having been surmounted; yet a very serious article still remains to be enquired into, viz. the *expence* necessary to support it. . . . Supposing the inhabitants of all these colonies amount to *three millions* — and I am of opinion that their number is not greater — each individual, man, woman, and child, black and white, would have *twenty shillings* sterling, i.e. about four Spanish dollars, to pay *annually* for defraying the public expence. . . .

Where the money is to come from which will defray this enormous annual expence of *three millions*, sterling, and all those other debts, I know not; unless the author of *Common Sense*, or some other ingenious projector, can discover the *Philosopher's Stone*, by which iron and other base metals may be transmuted into gold. Certain I am, that our commerce and agriculture, the two principal sources of our wealth, will not support such an expence. The whole of our exports from the Thirteen United Colonies in the year 1769, amounted only to £2,887,898 sterl.; which is not so much, by near half a million, as our annual expence would be, were we independent of Great Britain. Those exports, with no inconsiderable part of the profits arising from them, it is well known, centered finally in Britain, to pay the merchants and manufacturers there for goods we had imported thence, and yet left us still in debt! What then must our situation be, or what the state of trade, when oppressed with such a burthen of annual expence! When every article of commerce, every necessary of life, together with our lands, must be heavily taxed, to defray that expence!

Such is the load of debt and expence we should incur by this Writer's hopeful exchange of our connection with Great Britain, for independency and Republicanism! And all this, after being exhausted by a tedious war, and perhaps our shipping and seaports destroyed! This is a very serious matter; which is obvious to every understanding, and which no sophistry can evade. All who have any prudence or common sense left, or any property to lose, will pause and consider well, before they plunge themselves into such a dreadful situation. How little do those who desire this situation, know what they are about, or what they desire.

But here it may be said — *that all the evils above specified, are more tolerable than slavery.* With this sentiment I sincerely agree — any hardships, however great are preferable to slavery. But then I ask, is there no other alternative in the present case? Is there no choice left us but slavery, or those evils? I am confident there is; and that both may be equally avoided. Let us only shew a disposition to treat or negociate in earnest — let us fall upon some method to set a treaty or negociation with Great Britain on foot; and if once properly begun, there is a moral certainty that this unhappy dispute will be settled to the mutual satisfaction and interest of both countries. For my part, I have not the least doubt about it.

It would be improper and needless for me to enlarge on the particulars that should be adjusted at such a treaty. The maturest deliberation will be necessary on the occasion, as well as a generous regard to every part of the Empire. I shall just beg leave to suggest my opinion on a few points — I think America should insist, that the claim of parliamentary taxation be either explicitly relinquished; or else, such security given as the case will admit, and may be equivalent to a formal relinquishment, that this claim shall not be exerted. When this most important point is gained, America should consider, that there is a great difference between having her money wrested from her by others, and not giving any of it herself, when it is proper to give. While she is protected, and shares in the

advantages resulting from being a part of the British Empire,
she should contribute something for that protection and those
advantages; and, I never heard a sensible American deny this.
Moreover, she should stipulate for such a freedom of trade as
is consistent with the general welfare of the State; and that this
interesting object be settled in such a manner as to preclude, as
much as possible, any impolitic, or injurious infringements
hereafter. All this may be easily done, if both sides are only
disposed for peace, and there are many other particulars which
would be exceedingly beneficial to America, and might be
obtained, as they could not interfere with the interest of Great
Britain or any other part of the Empire. . . .

*   *   *

But it may be asked — what probability is there that Britain
will enter on such a treaty, or listen to proposals of this kind?
Is she not preparing for war, and fitting out a formidable
armament against the colonies? I answer — there is every
reason to believe that she will enter on such a treaty if it is
desired; and that she will listen to reasonable proposals. It is
her interest to do so. To hold these colonies by the sword
only, were she ever so powerful, would be holding them by a
very precarious, expensive tenure. Such a Union with the
Colonies as will promote their interest equally with her's, is
the only effectual way of attaching them to her. Is it reasonable to suppose that Great-Britain does not see this? Or that
she is not sensible of it? Besides, it has been openly and expressly declared in Parliament that *taxation is given up* by the
Ministry; we are also assured that some very respectable names
have been lately added to the advocates of America; and Commissioners have been appointed to treat with us. All these
things are in our favour, and promise a prosperous issue to a
negociation, if once begun. The British armament will not
in the least impede a treaty. Belligerent-Powers, when on the
eve of peace, always make as vigorous preparations for war, as
if there was no thought of peace. America also is preparing

for war, which is no more than a prudent step. It need not prevent her from treating; and she may therefore obtain better terms.

But a Declaration for Independency on the part of America, would preclude treaty intirely; and could answer no good purpose. We actually have already every advantage of independency, without its inconveniences. By a Declaration of Independency, we should instantly lose all assistance from our friends in England. It would stop their mouths; for were they to say anything in our favour, they would be deemed rebels, and treated accordingly.

Our author is much elated with the prospect of foreign succour, if we once declare ourselves Independent; and from thence promiseth us mighty matters. . . . The only European power from which we can possibly receive assistance, is France. But France is now at peace with Great-Britain; and is it probable that France would interrupt that peace, and hazard a war with the power which lately reduced her so low, from a *disinterested* motive of aiding and protecting these Colonies?

Consider this matter as you will, view the Declaration of Independency in what light you please; the ruin of America must be the inevitable consequence. Our author's earnestness and zeal therefore, that we should declare ourselves Independent, serves only to prove that he himself is desperate; and that he would gladly bring this whole continent into the same situation.

But our author repeatedly tells us — "That to expend so many millions for the sake of getting a few vile acts repealed, is unworthy of the charge." Now to pass over the gross insult here offered to the Continental Congress, who had this important object principally in view, in the spirited measures they have taken: I answer — That if five times as many millions have been expended, America would be an immense gainer, provided those acts are repealed, and her liberties, property, and trade, are settled on a firm basis, by a Constitutional Union with Great-Britain. Were that measure once

effected, the peace and prosperity of this continent would be
as immutably and certainly secure as anything in this world
can. We should be the happiest people in the world. The
Americans have fully evinced, to the conviction of the most
incredulous, that they have an high sense of their liberties, and
sufficient spirit to vindicate those liberties. Their numbers,
strength, and importance, will be daily increasing; these will
command respect from Great-Britain, and ensure to them a
mild and equitable treatment from her. She will not hereafter
be overanxious to contend, or come to blows with them. This
I think is clear to demonstration; and hence we may learn to
set a proper value on the rant which this author throws out,
as if America would be perpetually embroiled with England
hereafter, unless we declare for independency.

Let the spirit, design and motives which are undeniably evident in our respective pamphlets, decide which should be attended to most.

The author of *Common Sense* is a violent stickler for Democracy or Republicanism only — every other species of government is reprobated by him as tyrannical: *I* plead for that constitution which has been formed by the wisdom of ages — is
the admiration of mankind — is best adapted to the genius of
Britons, and is most friendly to liberty.

He takes pleasure in aggravating every circumstance of our
unhappy dispute — would inspire others with the same rage
that instigates himself, and would set his fellow subjects to
cutting each others throats. *I* would most gladly, were it in
my power, draw a veil of eternal oblivion over any errors
which Great Britain or the colonies may have fallen into —
I would willingly persuade them to mutual harmony and
union; since on these their mutual happiness and interest
depends.

He is evidently goaded on by ambition and resentment, to
seek for the gratification of those passions in an independent
republic here; which would reduce America to the same desperate state with himself; *I* have no interest to serve but what

is common to my countrymen — but what every American of property is concerned in equally with me.

He places himself at the head of a party; and spurns from him with the utmost contempt and indignation, all who will not enlist under his banner: *I* am of no party, but so far as the welfare of America is aimed at; and I believe there are many who aim at this in every party. I have not learned to pace with such intire acquiescence in the trammels of any party, as not to desert it, the moment it deserts the interests of my country.

He recommends a new, untried romantic scheme, at which we would at first have shuddered — which is big with inevitable ruin, and is the last stage of political phrenzy. *I* am for pursuing the same object, and acting on the same principles and plan with which we set out, when this contest began, and of whose success there is a moral certainty.

This, as far as I can know or see, is the true state of our case — let Heaven and Earth judge between us.

America is far from being yet in a desperate situation. I am confident she may obtain honourable and advantageous terms from Great Britain. A few years of peace will soon retrieve all her losses. She will rapidly advance to a state of maturity, whereby she may not only repay the parent state amply for all past benefits; but also lay under the greatest obligations. America, till very lately, has been the happiest country in the universe. Blest with all that nature could bestow with the profusest bounty, she enjoys besides, more liberty, greater privileges than any other land. How painful is it to reflect on these things, and to look forward to the gloomy prospects now before us! But it is not too late to hope that matters may mend. By prudent management her former happiness may again return; and continue to encrease for ages to come in a union with the parent state.

However distant humanity may wish the period; yet, in the rotation of human affairs a period may arrive, when (both countries being prepared for it) some terrible disaster, some dreadful convulsion in Great Britain, may transfer the seat of empire to this western hemisphere — where the British constitution, like the Phoenix from its parent's ashes, shall rise with youthful vigour and shine with redoubled splendor.

But if America should now mistake her real interest — if her sons, infatuated with romantic notions of conquest and empire, ere things are ripe, should adopt this republican scheme: They will infallibly destroy the smiling prospect. They will dismember this happy country — make it a scene of blood and slaughter and entail wretchedness and misery on millions yet unborn.

CHAPTER 5

Two
Revolutionary
Views

Once independence was declared, the loyalist was an obvious enemy to the new order. But the difficult question remained: how could the revolutionary tell a loyalist from an ordinary citizen?

Nathaniel Whitaker (1730–1795), born at Huntington, Long Island, was a contentious man by nature. A Presbyterian minister who was at odds with successive congregations over questions of church government, he was sufficiently diverse in his interests to establish a saltpeter factory at Salem during the war. He delivered a Jeremiad against the loyalists at the turn of 1777 from his pulpit in the Tabernacle Church, Salem. After expounding his Old Testament text, Whitaker called on his hearers to seek out and destroy the "un-American" Americans in their midst. He gave useful hints on how to spot traitors to the cause of liberty.

In contrast to Whitaker, Francis Hopkinson (1737–1791) favored a quieter approach. The son of one of the founders of the College of Philadelphia, he had been the first student registered there. He practiced law and developed considerable talents as a musician, composer, poet, and essayist. He was one of the signers of the Declaration of Independence, and held several offices under the Continental Congress during the war. His satire on the loyalists, written in 1777, showed the wide range of nefarious deeds popularly attributed to them.

NATHANIEL WHITAKER
An Antidote Against Toryism, Newburyport, John Mycall, 1777.
Text from a Salem reprint, 1811
pp. 3, 9, 20–25, 29–31

JUDGES V, 23

Curse ye Meroz, said the Angel of the Lord, curse ye bitterly
the inhabitants thereof, because they came not to the help of
the Lord, to the help of the Lord, against the mighty. . . .

* * *

From this view of the text and context, we may deduce the
following doctrinal observations.

  I. That the cause of Liberty is the cause of God and truth.
 II. That to take arms and repel force by force, when our
     Liberties are invaded, is well pleasing to God.
III. That it is lawful to levy war against those who oppress us,
     even when they are not in arms against us.
 IV. That indolence and backwardness in taking arms, and
     exerting ourselves in the service of our Country, when
     called thereto by the public voice in order to recover and
     secure our freedoms, is a heinous sin in the sight of God.
  V. That God requires a people, struggling for their Liberties,
     to treat such of the community who will not join them, as
     open enemies, and to reject them as unworthy the privileges
     which others enjoy. . . .

* * *

I fear there are many among us, in one disguise or other,
who when stript of their vizards, will appear to be of the
inhabitants of Meroz; . . . Among these characters I do not
include such as aid, or in words or actions defend, or openly
declare for the enemy, and plead the right of Great-Britain "to
bind us in all cases whatsoever," Of such there are not many

among us; owing probably to their fear of a vast majority, which is on the side of freedom; and therefore they put on the guise of friendship, while they endeavour secretly to work destruction to the cause. These may be known by the following marks.

1. Observe the man who will neither go himself, nor contribute of his substance (if able) to encourage others to go into the war. Such do what in them lays to break up the army: These incur the curse of Meroz.

2. Others will express wishes for our success, but will be sure to back them with doubts of the event, and fears of a heavier yoke. You may hear them frequently magnifying the power of the enemy, and telling of the *nine hundred chariots of iron;* the dreadful train of artillery, and the good discipline of the *British* troops — Of the intolerable hardships the soldiers undergo, and the starving condition of their families at home: And by a thousand such arts endeavouring to discourage the people from the war.

3. There are other pretended friends whose countenance bewrays them. When things go ill with our army, they appear with a cheerful countenance, and assume airs of importance, and you'll see the Core holding conference in one corner or another. The joy of their hearts on such occasions, will break thro' all disguises, and discover their real sentiments; while their grief and long faces on a reverse of fortune, is a plain index pointing to the end at which they really aim.

4. Others, who talk much for liberty, you will find ever opposing the measures of defence proposed; making objections to them, and shewing their inconsistency; while they offer none in their stead, or only such as tend to embarrass the main design: They are so prudent that they waste away days, yea months to consider; and are ever full of their wise cautions, but never zealous to execute any important project. . . . These *over* and *over* prudent men ought to be suspected, and viewed with a watchful eye: And the discerning mind will soon be

able to discover, whether such counsels spring from true wisdom, or from a design to ensnare.

5. Some are discovered by the company they keep. You may find them often with those who have given too much reason to suspect their enmity to our cause, and rarely with the zealous friends of liberty, except by accident; and then they speak and act like creatures out of their element, and soon leave the company, or grow mute, when *liberty* is the subject of the discourse.

6. There are others who in heart wish well to our cause, but through fear of the power of our enemies they are backward to join vigorously to support it; they really wish we might succeed, but they dread the hardships of a campaign, and choose so to conduct, that on whatever side victory may declare, they may be safe.

7. Others wish well to the public cause, but have a much greater value for their own private and personal interest. They are high sons of liberty, till her cause crosses their private views, and even then they boast in her name, while like George 3d. they stab her to the heart, by refusing submission to those regulations which are essential to her preservation.

All these, and many others of the like kind, might doubtless have been found in Meroz, and yet the best of them all fell under the bitter curse: . . .

* * *

The application of this to our present time is easy. The present war, 'tis probable, had never been commenced, had none of the inhabitants of Meroz been in our land; or if begun could not have been carried on to this day. On them, therefore, as the confederates, abettors and supporters of the tyrant, lies the guilt of this war. And as they are partners with him in the sin, so they ought to be involved in the punishment he deserves. If it is lawful to deprive the inhabitants of Great Britain of their property, when in our power, and convert it to our use; if this be a just retaliation for the injury they have

done us, and all too little to countervail the damage; much
more the interest of those who live among us, and yet assist
the enemy in their cruel designs, ought to be confiscated for
the service of the public, by how much more mischief have
they done and are capable of doing these States, and by how
much greater their sin. . . . The law of retaliation is sometimes
just and necessary, even when the persons offending are not
made the subjects of it; how much more when the trans-
gressors themselves are in our power? Nor can we do justice
to ourselves or the public, or to our brethren now suffering in
hard and cruel durance among the enemy; nor to our posterity;
nor lastly to the manes of our murdered friends who have
fallen in the field, or expired in loathsome prisons with cold
and hunger; till we inflict some just and exemplary punishment on those who had brought these calamities on us. . . .

*   *   *

This discourse also shows us how we ought to treat those
who do not join in the cause of freedom we have espoused.

1. As they are accursed of God, and we are commanded to
curse them, we ought at least to shun their company. What
a shame it is to see those born to freedom, and professing zeal
for her cause, associating themselves with the willing slaves
of an abandoned tyrant and murderer? O how do such debase
themselves, and give occasion to suspect them as belonging
to the same herd. But it may be asked, how shall they be distinguished from friends? Attend to the characters already
given, and you may see enough to justify you in avoiding in-
timacy with them; though they may so disguise that no
evidence appears to condemn them to open and condign
punishment. Happy would it be should our civil fathers draw
some determinate line of distinction between freemen and the
slaves of power. For want of this we have suffered greatly
already, and if this be not done, the consequences I fear will be
fatal.

2. As soon at they are discovered we ought to disarm them:

For as they will not assist us, we should put it out of their power to hurt us or our families, when we at any time shall be called to action. Yea,

3. As such forfeit all the privileges of freemen; their estates should be forfeited and applied to support the war; and themselves banished from these states. The curse we are commanded to inflict on the inhabitants of Meroz, must imply as much as this; and benevolence to millions demands this of us; not out of hatred to their persons, but their crimes, which strike at the life and happiness of these States. This punishment must be inflicted not by the people at large, but by our rulers, with whom, under God, we have entrusted our safety; and in whose wisdom we confide, to take proper vengeance on them in due time. But should this be delayed, without proper reasons assigned . . . we must look on [such delay] as another instance of divine displeasure, which speaks to all to search after, and by sincere repentance and thorough reformation, remove the moral cause of God's controversy with us.

When all this shall take place, we shall then see our councils filled with men inspired with wisdom to know what Israel ought to do; our arms victorious and triumphant; the inhabitants of Meroz justly punished: Peace, Liberty and Safety restored; the rod of tyranny broken; pure and undefiled religion prevailing, and the voice of joy and gladness echoing round our land. May God hasten this happy, happy day. And let all the people say, AMEN and Amen. —— . *Hallelujah.*

FRANCIS HOPKINSON
Two Letters *in Miscellaneous Essays and Occasional Writings,*
3 vols.
                    Philadelphia, T. Dobson, 1792, Vol. I, pp. 132–141

MR. PRINTER,

I am *a Tory,* the son of a Tory, born and bred in the pure principles of unconditional submission, and a true friend of the Hanoverian family — right or wrong and at all events. The king of England, is in my humble opinion, entitled, *jure divino*, to govern absolutely, not only the British empire, but the East and West Indies — not only the East and West Indies, but the continent of North America — not only these, but even the whole of this paltry world.

But the infatuated people of this most vile portion of this most vile planet, have been moved by the instigation of the Devil to oppose the earnest desire of George III — God bless his Majesty! — to govern them *in all cases whatsoever*, according to his good will and pleasure. For my own part, I truly abominate and abhor their rebellious obstinacy. His Majesty hath been pleased, in his great goodness, and to my unspeakable satisfaction, to send over his fleets and armies to conquer and subdue this horrible country. Now, it is the indispensable duty of all those who would be called the friends of arbitrary government and of the said George III, to render all the assistance in their power to the aforesaid fleets and armies, and to the worthy Lords and Generals, whom this just and benign monarch hath commissioned to direct and manage them.

Amongst the implements of war, the Pen and the Printing Press are not the most insignificant. It is true, they can break no bones — can shed no blood — but they can instigate men to do both: and by their influence over the minds of the multitude, can, perhaps, do more towards gaining a point, or opposing a purpose, than the sword or the bayonet. For this reason, I have anxiously desired to see a printing press in this city subservient to the purposes of Lord and General Howe; and it is with great satisfaction I find they have at last got a printer to their mind — one perfectly disposed to forward their humane designs. I was boasting, in the fulness of my heart, of *The Pennsylvania Ledger*, printed by Mr *Humphreys*, to a friend whom I supposed to be a tory like myself: but I had quite mistaken my man. He had the assurance to address me on the subject in the following manner. I will give it nearly in his own words, that you may see what dangerous characters we have amongst us.

It has been the policy of every government, [said he] from the beginning of time to this, when the honour, safety, and existence of that government depended on the fate of war, to use every possible means to forward and strengthen the efforts of its citizens and friends, and to counteract the force and subtlety of its enemies.

For this end, even under the most popular constitutions, many of the sacred rights of the people have been hard pressed and even suspended, and that without endangering the constitution, provided such extraordinary exertions of government be manifestly sanctioned by the necessity of the case. The British King, without even the plea of necessity impresses men for supplying his navy in time of war; a practice not authorized by the constitution, and a high infringement of the personal rights of the subject.

The liberty of the press has ever been justly esteemed as one of the most important popular privileges in a free government. It is indeed highly reasonable that the channels of information should be kept open and uncorrupted — and no man holds this right in more sacred estimation than I do. But when this privilege is manifestly abused, and the press becomes an engine in the hands of an enemy for sowing dangerous dissensions, spreading false alarms, and undermining the defensive operations of government in an hour of danger, ought not that government upon the undeniable principles of self-preservation, to silence, by its own authority, such an internal enemy to its peace and safety? — I have now in view *The Pennsylvania Ledger*, a paper manifestly in the interests of the enemy: whether we consider the complexion of the paper itself, or the known political character of the editor. Why should a dangerous lenity protect a man in the abuse of that very lenity which is his only security, and on which he so ungratefully presumes? or why should he, under the sanction of one right, be permitted to aim at the subversion of all the other rights of his country? Would not our council of safety be very justifiable in silencing a press, whose weekly productions insult the feelings of the people, and are so openly inimical to the American cause?

Did you ever hear such a fellow? For my part I was so shocked at his principles, that I left him abruptly, and am determined to have no more communication with him.

Mr. Printer,

It is not easy to conceive how much I was surprised and disappointed at the discourse of my friend, as communicated to you in my last. There are indeed some whom we confide in with safety in these precarious times: and people should be very cautious in opening their minds before persons of a doubtful political character.

It is a rule in our tory society to be very circumspect in this particular — but I confess that, in this instance, I was not as prudent as I should have been; and I have had the mortification of being reprimanded for my indiscretion before a full meeting.

You can hardly imagine what regularity prevails in our board of tories. We are all formed into committees of various denominations, and appointed to various duties. I have myself the honour to belong to *the committee of wiles and stratagems.* It was I, Mr. Printer, who planned the scheme for stealing the mail sent by General Washington to congress.* — And my design was so successfully executed, that whilst the committee of congress were searching Bristol for those letters, they were then on their way to our friend, *General Howe;* where they safely arrived, as we have been since informed. You may be sure that I gained great applause for this manoeuvre.

We have also a *committee of false reports; —* whose duty is to fabricate and publish such articles of intelligence as may tend to alarm and terrify timid whigs, and distract the minds of the people. These are circulated at such times as the situation of public affairs may make them most probable. Sometimes they are thrown out in whispers, in so dark and secret a man-

---

* By this Mail (which was stole from off the express horse, whilst he was refreshing himself at Bristol) Gen. Howe was informed of the situation of the American army, and of the day on which most of the troops would be disbanded by the expiration of their enlistments. He accordingly came into Jersey with his whole force at the critical time and drove Gen. Washington over the Delaware.

ner that their origin cannot be traced; and at other times openly, by means of the *Pennsylvania Ledger.*

We have, moreover, a *committee of true intelligence;* whose business it is to employ a number of spies, who are directed to mix amongst the people in the assumed character of zealous whigs; to hire themselves as servants and waiters in houses and taverns frequented by members of congress. This committee holds a regular correspondence with our friends in the British army; so that we are certainly informed of what passes on both sides, from the best authority, and are thereby enabled to take all advantages. Happily for us, the several ferries and stages have as yet been left free and open, so that our messengers pass and re-pass without examination, and of consequence this department has been attended with little or no difficulty.

Another committee is called the *committee of lies;* whose duty differs from that of *false reports* in this — the latter is to circulate misrepresentations of facts respecting the armies, and things of a public nature, on the large scale: whilst the former only frame temporary lies for the use of this city: particularly respecting the deliberations and intentions of congress. These lies must be fresh and fresh every day; and always supported by a strong assertion that the information came from some leaky member of congress; generally without mentioning the name of any individual member; yet, in cases of urgency, the real name of some leading character may be adduced; when the lie may have had its operation before it can be contradicted.

There is likewise a *committee of extortion;* these are wealthy men, who monopolize, as far as they can, the articles most wanted for the rebel army; buy up the necessaries of life, and put on them the highest prices they can with any appearance of propriety, in order to make the people discontented and uneasy.

The last committee I shall mention is *the committee of depreciation — as important as any —* they are to take all possible pains, and to exercise very subtile art to run down and depreciate the Continental currency. This committee is very large, and composed chiefly of brokers and monied men. They get some of this money, and run with it to discharge any debts they may have contracted, with a seeming anxiety to get rid of it as fast as possible. If they have goods for sale, they openly avow three prices: one, if the purchaser will agree to pay in hard money; an higher price, if in provincial paper, under the old government; and a still higher, if in the present continental bills of credit. But we have many other ways of bringing that currency into disrepute, which I am not at liberty to mention.

I would give a list of the men of most influence in our society — at present this would be improper: but I will be more explicit hereafter, when *toryism* may be more safely and openly avowed.

Some narrow minded people say, that we are doing all we can to ruin our country, and entail a miserable slavery on our unborn posterity. We believe we are doing the best we can for ourselves — and pray what has posterity done for us, that we should run the risk of confiscation and a halter for them? Our fixed opinion is, that the British army must eventually subdue this country — and setting the right or wrong of the thing out of the question, we think we may as well have the reputation and advantage of assisting them in their designs as not. 'Tis true, if the British Generals should succeed in their enterprise we may see our neighbours and friends imprisoned by hundreds, and hanged by dozens; their estates confiscated, and their children turned out to beggary and want; but then we shall ourselves escape, and enjoy in safety our lives and estates — and, perhaps, be even promoted, for our present services, to places of honour and emolument.

I am, &c.

A TORY.

CHAPTER 6 Resignation and Revenge

After five years of warfare and the intervention of assorted European powers, no end was in sight. The very survival of the United States defied all the expectations of the loyalists, and every month that passed increased the possibility that independence would triumph.

One unhappy observer of these events was the historian of New York, William Smith (1728–1793). A Yale graduate, lawyer, and member of the council, he had been very active in New York politics before the war. Although most of his friends became revolutionaries, Smith decided to remain loyal, was appointed chief justice of the colony, and in 1786 became chief justice of Quebec. His *Candid Retrospect* was an historical review written more in sadness than in anger. He tried to strike a balance of rights and wrongs between mother country and colonies, accepting as valid all the colonial grievances normally taken to justify the Revolution, but stopping short at the point where opposition led to a war that could destroy the whole empire. However, there was apparently little comfort to be drawn from apportioning past blame, and the pamphlet concluded with more than a hint of resignation to the appalling possibility of American independence.

The American war ended in 1782 with a cease-fire, and almost a year elapsed before the signing of the peace treaty. Many loyalists, apparently unaware of the depths of feeling aroused in their fellow-countrymen, considered returning to their homes at this time. For some of the more prominent, including two of the contributors to this volume, the welcome awaiting was spelled out in no uncertain terms.

WILLIAM   SMITH

The Candid Retrospect, or the American War examined by Whig Principles, Charleston, S. C., John Wells Jr., 1780.

Reprinted New York, Rivington, 1780.
Text from Charleston edition.

The political creed of America (for I make no estimate of two parties, who taken together are a *Minority* of the continent) may be comprised in the twelve following articles.

I. Every nation has authority to frame such a government for itself, as will, without injury to others, be most conducive to its own felicity.

II. The national sovereignty under every form of government, whether in the hands of one, or of many persons, or however modelled, is absolute; for no State can exist, if any of its members may by force or fraud attempt its subversion with impunity: And therefore, every nation punishes treason, or an attempt tending to overturn the constitution, as the highest crime of which a subject can be guilty.

III. No man can be innocent, even *Foro Conscientiae*, in an endeavour to change the government of his country, if the meditated revolution will light up a civil war, and the miseries in prospect are likely to exceed those, which the community have been accustomed to endure.

IV. The establishments made in America by English emigrants and their associates, *might* in the early days of the colonies, if the parent country had so determined, have been prevented or broken up.

V. The Lords and Commons of England, being cognisant of the grants and charters of their Kings and Queens, for the encouragement of the Colonies, and of the transactions under them; and afterwards co-operating for regulating the plantations, rendering them secure against foreign invasions and useful to Great-Britain, they cannot be considered as *merely Royal*, but Parliamentary, or national establishments.

VI. The grants and charters of the colonies, and the posterior settlements, regulations and usages by the permission, and with the knowledge or privity, and without the interdiction of Parliament, are incontestible proofs of a great national covenant between the Mother Country and the Colonies; for her favours (which undeniably have been many and great) by inspiring the Colonists with confidence, and exposing them to hazardous and expensive undertakings, created rights; and gratitude never obliges to returns and surrenders, incompatible with those rights which are essential to the felicity of the receiver of the benefits.

VII. Before the years 1764 the King, Lords and Commons, were universally acknowledged to be the supreme law-givers of the whole empire; of which the Colonies were members.

VIII. The national covenant bound the parent country to protect and promote the Colonies, according to the good faith implied in the grants and charters, and other royal and national acts in their favour, as far as was consistent with the general weal of all the dispersions of the nation; and it obliged the plantations to submit to her authority, in all cases not repugnant to their grants, charters and establishments; and to such acts and contributions, as were necessary for the *common* defence and felicity of the empire.

IX. Neither of the contracting parties may dissolve this compact, as long as their joint aim in the union, to wit, *their mutual* prosperity, can be attained by it.

X. As no provision was made for constituting an impartial Judge between them, to bridle or correct the partiality or infidelity of either party, therefore their controversies are to be decided by negotiation and treaty, or on appeal by battle to the Lord of Hosts; for neither is obliged to surrender its

essential rights at the *will* of the other, and each is justifiable
in exerting its own self-preserving powers.

XI. When one of them wants either will or ability to fulfil
its engagements, the other, if not instrumental to this disaffection, will be discharged from the original obligation. But,

XII. Since amongst imperfect beings offences are inevitable,
the contractors are by the laws of a judge who cannot be
deceived, reciprocally bound, upon exceptions taken, to pursue
every measure of a reconciliatory nature, consistent with the
end of the union; and to such mutual condescensions, as tend
to the re-establishment of the general felicity, peace and harmony: And this is the more eminently their duty, since the
empire consists of *other* branches, which have offended neither
of the parties at strife, and will nevertheless be ruined if the
controversy ends in a separation.

In the application of these principles to the present quarrel,
perhaps neither Great-Britain nor America, will appear to be
without blame.

What a new and awful idea of the constitution did the
Parent Country hold up to her Colonies, at the passing of the
stamp act! Her language was this:

You Americans are absolutely ours. We may dispose of your
persons, your commerce, your lands and acquisitions as we
please. You have no rights. The grants of our Kings to your
ancestors, do not bind this nation. The privileges and securities
of Englishmen cannot be yours unless you return to the old
realm. Our ancient indulgences were *temporary* permissions,
from which you can deduce no title to *permanent* enjoyments.
Your plea that our Commons are not of your electing, and that
we and they are interested in the increase of your burdens, can
come with propriety only from the mouth of a British inhabitant. — All America is subject to our taxations; nor will we hear
your complaints, until you first own our authority to deal with
you as we please, and acknowledge that such benefits as you
request, are to be expected not as of right, but of grace.

Had England such principles at the first emigrations, she was bound to declare them to the adventurers, before they gave themselves to the winds and the seas, to gain her a share of the wealth and commerce of the new world, by which her island has been converted into a *Nation of Princes*.

But this she never did speak until this memorable aera; and therefore the Colonies were in consternation at the haughty tone, uttering this novel explanation of the nature of the union. They remonstrated — they resisted — and the instant Great-Britain took off the new burden, America, regarding her *deeds* more than her words, submitted without cavalling, to that rational sovereignty she had formerly exercised, to the common advantage of the empire.

The grand desideratum of the moment in which the stamp act was repealed (1766) was some plan for obtaining in future, the reasonable contributions of the Colonies for the *common defence* consistent with the supremacy of Parliament and the freedom of America, either in the old or in some new and unexceptionable mode — If assemblies were *no longer* to be trusted, for grants on separate requisitions from the Crown (though the Colonies had in this way the credit of having overacted their parts) an American Parliament might have been constituted to *insure* and *quicken* the supplies; or permanent funds might have been set apart in every plantation, for their quota's to the national charge, rising and falling with the commerce of a Colony, perfectly consistent with *their* safety and the *national supremacy*, and requisite for the union and direction of their force: But to the astonishment of commonsense, Great Britain, blind to futurity, and anxious only for present peace, contented herself with an empty declaration of her authority to bind the Colonies *in all cases whatsoever;* and as if this would have prevented America from indulging jealousies, or have induced her to slide into security and confidence, she absurdly enrolled it among her laws. — Easy themselves, the ministers of the day, devised nothing to counteract

the poison administered by their predecessors, and seemed to
be regardless of the durable interests of the Monarch they
served, and the nation who resigned to their counsels. — But
to proceed, we remark,

1. That the present animosities are imputable to the pride
and avarice of Great-Britain, in assuming an authority, inconsistent with the compact by which the empire had been long
prosperously united. The Colonies had the merit of returning
to their submission, as soon as they were disburdened of the
stamp duties, the irritating assertion of a right to despotick
sovereignty over them notwithstanding. They remained quiet
till Mr. Townshend revived the old claim in a new form, by
imposing duties upon paper, paint, &c. for raising a revenue,
subversive of the Colony Legislatures and the ancient customs
of the Empire.

2. That the Colonies were justifiable in censuring the new
law devised to execute the tea duty act; for that aiming to
inforce the claim of absolute sovereignty obliged to some
conduct or declaration against an unconditional submission —
Perhaps it justified the open violation to which they resorted.
— Representations and petitions having been tried without
effect, what could be expected from the mere influences of
dissuasions against the purchase of the duted article? Had not
the patriot dissuader to apprehend prosecution and ruin unless
when imprisoned, his countrymen would rise up against the
government for his redemption? And which measure was least
exceptionable, the destruction of the commodity, or the
rupture of gaols, for a deliverance of the prisoners in the confederacy, and the sudden overturning of the Colony Government for defeating the *regular* course of the law?

3. That the resentment of Great-Britain, on the destruction
and expulsion of the tea cargoes, manifested in the coercive
measures of 1774, by altering the charter of the Massachu-
sett's Bay, extinguishing the commerce of Boston, collecting

an army there, rendering the soldiery dispunishable for the shedding of blood, modelling the province of Quebeck favourable to the designs of compulsion and violence, was utterly unjustifiable, and an infraction of the league, which obliged Great-Britain to protect the Colonies; and these severities were the more inexcusable, since to that moment her sovereignty in *all cases* (the matter of taxation excepted) had not been denied by the Colonies; but was by all their courts, and in all their proceedings, confessed or implied, adjudged *and* supported.

4. That the provinces were not blameable in forming a Congress, to unite their counsels and ward off danger, as they did in September, 1774.

5. That it was the duty of the American Assemblies, and of the Congress acting for the whole continent, *at that* time to tender a plan to the Mother Country, for restoring peace, consistent with the compact, by which the Parliament of Great-Britain was to enjoy a supremacy for the common felicity of the empire; and consequently, that the declaration they then made, of the right of the Colonies to an *exclusive legislation*, not only in cases of taxation but of *internal polity*, subject only to the negative of their sovereign, was a departure in terms from the original league; since it left no authority to the Parliament of Great-Britain over the Plantations, except for the regulation of the *external* commerce of the Empire; and gave vigour to the jealousy *before* excited, by the misrepresentations of their enemies, of a design to maintain an inauspicious union and confederacy with the *Monarchs*, and not with the *Legislature and People* of Great-Britain; and that the intimation of the same Congress, of the willingness of the Colonies, to acquiesce in their condition *prior to* 1763, gave Great-Britain no sufficient ground to expect their submission, to the ancient acknowledged claims of her Parliament; since the repeal of the offensive statutes, *without a retraction* of the denial of her legislative authority, would, by a violent implication, establish the *Congress's declaration*, and amount to a

consent, that America was thenceforth to be the Ally of Great-Britain, and not what the Congress at *that very time*, averred her to be, a Member of the Empire.

6. That it would not have been inconsistent with the dignity of Great-Britain, if instead of declaring war against her Colonies, as in the joint address of the Lords and Commons to the King in January, 1775, she had animadverted upon the denial of her authority in all cases respecting internal polity, as *an error;* and have specified in what particulars the Americans should be restored to a *uti possidetis* relative to their charters, patents, assemblies, elections, and modes of government, &c. on condition of their contributing to the necessities of the Empire. And that the parliamentary vote of the 20th of February, 1775, would have more naturally effected a treaty of reconciliation, had it *explicitly* asserted, that the right reserved to Parliament, of *approving* the quantum of the Colony contributions towards the common defence, was not claimed upon the supposition, that Parliament authoritatively command levies, but only on her right to judge of the exercise or defect of a due sympathy in any branch of the empire, to the general necessities of the whole body; and especially if Great-Britain had at the same time, intimated a readiness to consent to such checks, limitations and restraints, as might be necessary to insure the application of them, to the end for which they were given; and had with these, promised a restitution of rights and an *act of oblivion.*

7. That it was a fault to issue that proposal, in terms *capable* of being construed, into an attachment to the principle of unlimited submission, and accompanying it with acts for augmenting her force at Boston, and restraining the fishery and commerce of her Colonies, and for neglecting to command a cessation of arms, until the Colonies had an opportunity to deliberate, with composure of mind, upon that proposal — more especially for her irritating sally to Concord and Lexington, on the 19th of April 1775, when no Governour but Mr. Gage, had received the Parliament's *conciliatory resolve.*

8. That as this vote, under these circumstances, and the partial direction of her wrath against the New-England Colonies, favoured the opinion of its being contrived, to deceive and divide the Provinces, the Congress of 1775, had some pretext for flying to arms, to repel further incursions of the British troops, till Government gave them an opportunity, in a condition less alarming, to explain the declaration of 1774 into a *consistency* with the ancient supremacy of *Parliament*, and to state the limitations requisite for their safety, in answer to the February resolution or proposal.

9. That the total rejection of it in August 1775, and the neglect of the Congress to recall or explain the declaration of 1774, had a natural tendency to exasperate the nation; and as the Continental successes in Canada, and the impotent state of the British army at Boston, did leave America in a condition, for a more cool and deliberate consideration of the controversy, than could have been expected *immediately* after the irritations at Lexington, Concord, and Charlestown, her Congress deserves the charge of abandoning to passion, if not to motives less excusable; it being then the palpable duty of both countries, by proper agents in a confidential way, to state and explain their respective claims and desires.

10. That the neglect of Great-Britain to supersede the orders to the navy, for sacrificing every town on the American coast, which should prepare for defence; and her continuance of hostilities after the petition to the King, preferred by Mr. Richard Penn in August 1775, submitting it to his wisdom to point to some plan for the restoration of harmony, confirmed the charge of her commencing a war to maintain an illiberal dominion.

11. That the Congress would have had merit with their countrymen, if instead of referring it to the King to direct "to a mode, by which the united applications of his faithful Colonists to the throne, in pursuance of their common councils, may be improved into a happy and permanent reconciliation"; they had at the same time expressly assured his

Majesty, that they meant not by their *declaration of rights* in 1774, to *exclude* Parliament from participating in the regulations respecting the *internal* polity of the Colonies: And that an omission so naturally confirming the suspicion of a design to involve the Empire in blood, by a struggle for dismembring it, discovers *at least* great imperfection in the counsels of that Congress; as it was reasonable to suppose, that the petition would be compared, with the principles and temper manifested in the preparations for an offensive war into Canada, and the disdainful rejection of the Parliament's proposal, of the month of February preceding.

12. That every partial view, whether of Great-Britain, to aggrandize herself by extortionate exactions from the Plantations, regardless of their felicity; or of America, to figure as an independent power, on the ruins of Great-Britain, Ireland, and the other Colonies, Factories and Settlements, is unrighteous in the sight of God; and upon the belief of the manifestation of his justice in the government of nations, must expose to the correction of his irresistable and unerring hand.

13. Both countries being chargeable with inattention to the obligations they were under to pursue the measures requisite to a reconciliation, neither of them could reject terms consistent with the *original compact*, though no reimbursements were offered for the losses they had sustained. Add to this, that the controversy arose from — neglect in our *early* days, to concert such specifick stipulations, as were necessary to prevent doubts and strife, and reconcile the safety of the Colonies with the general supremacy of Parliament; and that a definitive treaty restoring each country to a situation preferable to her primitive condition, afforded a reasonable security for her future felicity; Great-Britain's best hopes being founded on the dependence and union of America; and the Colonies being arrived at such a maturity of strength, as to command upon the principles of utility, a system of liberality, in the future management of their affairs.

14. That Great-Britain even in passing the *prohibitory act* of December 1775, opened a door to pacification, as it repealed the Boston port act, and the two other coercive statutes for restraining the fishery and the commerce of the Colonies; and enabled the Crown to appoint Commissioners, to render the *prohibiting act itself useless*, upon a treaty to be made with the Colonies, or with any port or place within either of them; and more especially as the King's Ministers had so early as September (soon after the Congress's petition to the King) dispatched messengers, who in *January* 1776, had interviews with certain of the Delegates at Philadelphia, and had such intimations, as gave just ground to hope for an immediate termination of all differences, had the Congress sent others on their parts, to confess *their* willingness to *negotiate* upon the overtures, which Administration (then supposed by the Colonies or their Congress to have the lead of Parliament) stood ready to recommend to the national approbation.

15. That the concealment of these pre-intimations so explanatory of the *true intent* of the armaments expected in June and July, 1776, and of the nature of the commission and instructions given to Lord and General Howe, added to the guilt of the Congress, and favoured the perilous design of drawing the people into the precipitate renunciation of the dependency of the Colonies, the 4th of July, 1776, and of plunging their countrymen into a tedious and desolating war.

16. That there is reason to suspect, that the views which prompted to that awful resolution, will lead the Delegates to practise every artifice, to hide its horrible tendency from the eye of the publick; and if possible, to turn the quarrel to their own emolument, at the expense of the blood and treasure of their country.

17. That the appeal being made by the sword to the Omniscient Judge, who will decide upon it with infallible rectitude, and the war wasting the empire, and tending to a separation ruinous to millions, who have taken *no part in the*

controversy, it concerns those who began, as well as those who support and protract it, under the loud calls of justice, humanity, benevolence, honour, religion and the general interest, to cultivate concord, and a return to their ancient union, according to that compact which eminently advanced the common prosperity, antecedent to the year 1764; for no end however laudable and desirable, will justify a perfidious and ambitious violation of that covenant, under which the two countries were placed by the Providence of God, be the prospect never so flattering to our zeal for the civil or religious interests of mankind; it being the indispensable duty of christians, to seek for *temporal* as well as *eternal* felicity in the way of well-doing; trusting it to the Supreme Ruler, to accomplish his benevolent designs, relating both to Church and State, according to his own infinite wisdom and uncontroulable sovereignty.

18. If it was the duty of the Congress by withholding at first or afterwards retracting the declaration of 1774, which renounces the whole authority of Parliament in the concerns of *civil polity*, to have prevented an open war; or to have terminated it by messages in answer to the overtures of January 1776, when but few of the Colonies had thought of even *temporary* establishments for *common* order, nor any of them had authorized their Delegates to vote for a disunion, or to have checked the military operations, by calling for the terms brought out by Lord Howe, and submitting them, under a cessation of arms, to the consideration of their constituents in autumn 1776, no subsequent transaction of the Congress, to give success to the unwarrantable project for dismembring the Empire, *then concealed from the multitude*, can bind the rest of their countrymen, in honour or conscience, to support a weak and wicked faction, in an obstinate prosecution of the war.

19. Who then are the real enemies of America, if not *they* who have perverted the *virtuous aims* of the *main body* of the people for the defence of their rights and priviledges, into

a war for dominion? And *seduced* some, *terrified* many, and
driven more, to assist in this extravagant enterprize — who,
under the disguise of patriot zeal, did, *unauthorized*, dispatch
an emissary [Silas Deane] in the winter 1776, to draw the
ancient enmity of France into a contention purely domestick;
and have since by various arts and assiduous labours, in and
out of Congress, opposed all peaceful negotiations, and effected
a league with the common foe, to gratify the corrupt aims of
private ambition and interest; and together with others, in
divers posts, offices and employments, are feeding and thriving
upon the miseries of their countrymen, and by force and fraud
preventing their return to the blessings of peace, liberty and
safety, under a most generous plan tendered by Great-Britain,
with proposals of a solemn convention, for advancing and
perpetuating the prosperity of the whole Empire?

20. It being manifest that nothing will satisfy the directors
of the American Councils (by whom several of the Colonies
suffer themselves to be ruled) but measures incompatible with
the safety of the many millions of the same natural stock with
themselves in Europe, Asia and Africa, and in the contented
dispersions in the Islands, as well as on the continent of America, Great-Britain will be justifiable in exerting the powers she
enjoys for her preservation, to render the rebelled Plantations
as *impotent* as they appear to be *unfriendly*, to the welfare of
that vast community, with whom they may be, as they once
were, happily united; and from whom they are now sullenly
severed, upon principles of partiality, reprobated by great
multitudes of their own countrymen, who have suffered insults, imprisonments, fines, sequestrations, and many of them
death itself.

21. But since men's passions became inflamed, under erroneous views of the measures requisite to promote and secure the
common interests of both countries, and it is scarce possible
for the ordinary tribunals of justice, biassed as they may be by
prejudices, *exactly* to discern the line of separation, between
that conduct, which from the motives and ends of the agent,

may not deserve blame, and a behaviour in the eye of the law
criminal and treasonable, it was wise and just, as well as merci-
ful in Great-Britain, to issue as she did in October, 1778,
general and undistinguishing pardons; that punishment might
be inflicted only for guilt to be contracted in *future,* by per-
severing in a conflict, undoubtedly degenerated from a struggle
for liberty, into an UNNATURAL REBELLION.

22. That the sufferings of the loyalists in all parts of the
continent, from the hands of fellow subjects, who while violating the rights of private judgment, are nevertheless appealing
in their fasts, prayers and thanksgivings, to the God of love
and mercy, for their innocence, will eternally demonstrate the
hypocrisy, avarice and profligacy of some, and the fanaticism
of the rest of their oppressors; as the forbearance of Great-
Britain, in not having yet executed a single rebel in her power,
and in restraining from the devastations and complicated
calamities, she might have brought upon the avowed ally of
her inveterate enemy, is of her lenity and generosity: And that
it will become her in future, to have a tender regard, not
only to her friends in America, but to discriminate the ignorant,
the timid, the helpless, the uninformed and the seduced, by
proportionable indulgences; and to remember at the final
termination of the war in a re-union, the fidelity and affection
she found here, and to strike hands with the Colonies, in a
free and generous establishment of their privileges, bought by
the blood of the *American,* as well as the *European* loyalist.

Lastly, That Great-Britain independent of her own interest
in the controversy, is, all circumstances considered, bound by
justice and honour to prevent the ruin of her American
friends, at every risk short of certain destruction to herself:
And that it will be her duty, if compelled by adversity to
conclude a disadvantageous peace, and to part with one or
more of her Colonies to France, Spain or any other foreign
nation, to stipulate in clear and strong terms, in behalf of the
loyalists who may be found there, for every advantage of dis-
posing of their estates, and free liberty to remove to such of

the Colonies or Dominions, as may not be unfortunately sur-
rendered at the end of the war, to a popish or arbitrary power.

ANONYMOUS
Open letter to William Smith, Charles Inglis &c., by Cives.
Dated State of New York
10th July 1783, [no title page]

To our ineffable astonishment, we are told that several of
you wish and mean to throw yourselves on the mercy of your
country! Be assured that such recreant conduct, can be
equalled by nothing but your former insolence, treachery and
cruelty — It has long been a received maxim, that tyrants are
dastards — you are, if our information be true, living monu-
ments of the truth of the assertion.

Is it possible that you, Mr. Smith, who have treated every
effort of the States to save themselves from the worst of des-
potisms, with the utmost contempt and ridicule, should now
wish to become a member of a society that you always held in
derision — a society that you strained every nerve to crush &
to annihilate! We cannot take a serious and impartial retrospect of your conduct, from the era of the Stamp-Act, without
suspecting that you are encouraged in this scheme by your
patrons the King and Ministry of Great-Britain, who mean
to use their whole influence against the confederacy of the
States, as well as against the alliance with France; especially
when we reflect on the high esteem you have been held in by
all the British commanders, and the particular attention they
have paid you; they reposing a trust & confidence in your
abilities, for chicanery, dissimulation, intrigue, hypocrysy and
loyalty; in composing of lies, fabricating pardons, and manu-
facturing memorials; have bribed you again to risk your life
in their Service, by a pretending submission and reconciliation
to your country; that you may, whenever opportunity offers,
deceive, betray and divide — Is it the policy of Britain, to

retain secret emissaries at every court in Europe, or their own writers, as well as others, do them injustice.

We are entirely at a loss to account for the delusion you seem to be under, Sir, unless it be the effect of your long practised impositions on the British, that have taught you to impose on yourself — Surely it cannot be your profession as a lawyer and civilian, that led you to imagine that governments founded like these, on the principles of equal liberty, could not be established, there being neither forms nor precedents for them, that has induced you vainly to believe that your profound knowledge in gubernatorial affairs would atone for your unparallelled machinations and treachery! nor can it be supposed that the declaration made to the Legislature of this State should have slipp'd so retentive a memory of your being an enemy to the Independence of the United States, and affirming that they never would be able to support it. Or does the same evil genius which guided you in the adoption of your party, still direct your choice?

If you mean to rely on your numerous and wealthy connexions in the country, as the wall of your preservation, you may be assured of having but a very slender support — the event of the revolution has not been so favourable to them as they wished or as they might have made it had they not, at least some of them, been activated partly by your own dastardly principles; that is, a love of riches and a lust of power, and even of those who had first joined the country, several have proved traitors, and others behaved so inconsistently, that they are generally held in contempt: And, if I may be allowed the expression, the political character of the whole, has rather suffered a retrograde improvement — Their quantum of wealth, and their arrogance of disposition, make them deservedly the objects of popular jealousy; the truth of which is evident, from the late elections — not one of them fills a government post, where the choice depends upon the suffrages of the people — Should you place your safety on such a paltry foundation as the influence of your friends, and former reputation, you will be convinced, when too late, of the inability of the one, and insignificancy of the other, to withstand the united force of a justly incensed multitude — . . . the good people of this State view you with indignation — you have deceived them, and they term you a hypocrite — they no longer consider you as that good man you once appeared to be — the affectation of uniting religion with your politicks, they justly charge as an insult to the Deity, and they reason very properly — Can the man who has deceived his country; can he who relinquished the society of which he was a member, to adhere to its enemies; can he who has machinated the most bloody designs against a country that gave him birth; can such a man be said to be the imitator of the divine Governor of the Universe, whose actions are guided by unerring rectitude and justice? The picture chills them with horror, and they turn from it with disgust.

And you Mr. Inglis: be pleased reverend Sir, permit us to approach you with all the respect due to the sacredness of your character, which had not you profaned and 'worn into vileness', would indeed have been truly venerable — but forgetting, or stifling thro' bigotry and resentment, the divine precepts of your mission, You, at an early period of our struggle, took a very active and vindictive part against your country — besides the many false and scurrilous pieces you wrote and published in Rivington's and Gaine's papers, in conjunction with your brother apostates Cooper and Vardill, against it, you, in a sermon adapted to the bloody designs of the author, expressly and explicitly called on the British grenadiers, to 'cut the Gordian knot', or in other words, the throats, of all who were opposed to the high-church government you laboured to establish — It is also no less surprising than certain, that you descended from the dignity of your station, and inhumanly insulted the misfortunes of individuals thrown into the hands of the enemy by the fate of war, and confined in loathsome dungeons. — Was this done like an apostle of the 'Holy Jesus?' Is such conduct consonant to the meek doctrines of the sacred religion you profess? . . . And can you now, be either so mean or stupid as to imagine that you will be suffered to reside in a country whose blood you have thus treacherously and cruelly contributed to spill in such wanton Profusion? Have you too, the arrogance to add insult to injury, and wish to seek an asylum among a people you so lately exerted yourself to destroy? If you have, remember destruction awaits you — nor can your sacredotal character protect you, even at the horns of the altar, from the just resentment of an injured and insulted people, some of whom tho' Episcopalians, are not the less your enemies; nor will any of those of your function, who have adopted a similar conduct meet with any more favour. . . .

Permit us now to address you individually and collectively — money may silence a judge, or it may put an attorney's tongue in motion, but it cannot stifle the honest resentment of virtuous Citizens, whose very looks will pierce your dastardly souls with convulsive anguish.

Were riches to determine the fate of their possessors, then have you made the most prudent choice, in adhering to the enemies of your country — but we wish shortly, to see the day, when, should you either meanly, arrogantly or insolently attempt to remain in the State, your basely gotten gains will only contribute to your condign punishment.

You certainly could never have entertained a single idea of continuing in this country, without supposing administration as base and corrupt as yourselves, and that they were ready to perjure themselves whenever opportunity offered, to participate of the fruits of your treachery — but thanks to a gracious Providence, it is not a British administration you have to settle the affair with, or there would be little doubt of your success.

If your minds were the thousandth part as susceptible of truth as falsehood or imposture, very little argument must convince you, or others in your situation, that the united force of friends, former reputation and riches, will not preserve you from the just resentment of an injured multitude. If you therefore are prudent, pass from this Land of Freedom, to that country whose politics and principles you have adopted, and whose servants you most assuredly are — If you are proud, do not meanly wait for the insults of a successful people; we do not harbour even a wish, that a page of history should be stained with a recital of your extrajudicial punishments: and that tho' you died justly, it was by the hands of your Fellow-citizens, who sacrificed you to the manes of their starved and murdered friends and relations, whose meager corpses, after lying many days publicly exposed in piles, (Funeral piles!) have been most inhumanly cast into sloughs or hollows, without sufficient earth to prevent the dogs from mangling them.

If you are not 'reserved for the day of destruction,' follow those who have set you a manly example — it is the heighth of folly for you to expect a recovery of your forfeited estates — this State has suffered too much ever to restore them — it has been the seat of the war, & you have been some of the principal encouragers of the enemy, to persist in reducing it even to depopulation and laying it waste — The war was begun at your request, and has been prolonged by your advice: it is therefore but common justice, that your estates should go to the support of it.

Finally, it is said that you have all combined, in conjunction with the foreign Tories, now with you, to keep out of the City [New York] as many of the true Whigs as possible, by which means, as you have murdered many others, you imagine, that you will be able to stem the torrent of public resentment, and turn the course of trade wholly to the British channel. There you are out again! For, if any assistance is requisite, thousands in the Counties, and the other States, stand ready to give it, the moment it is wanted; which it will not be, should the whole of you stay, and your allies also. Not that we mean to reject all Foreigners, but only such as came over at a certain period and extended the views of the British court to enslave the States — These must expect to make room for better company. . . .

PART THREE

General
Indictment
CHAPTER 7
and
Special Pleading

For men such as Nathaniel Whitaker, the return of peace held a real danger: the joyful victors might be soft on the loyalists. In a sermon of May 1783, Whitaker once again called for vigilance against the enemy within and the enemy without, now clamoring to return. If the loyalists within were to be allowed to remain, many of them would have to be deprived of their civil rights. For those without, no quarter need be asked; once readmitted they would form a fifth column to advance Britain's continuing evil designs.

Not all loyalists had been loyalists by choice, especially men caught in the ebb and flow of the contending armies. South Carolina was one of the states where a temporary British occupation had faced residents with the need to collaborate. In the circumstances, it was impossible to distinguish between those who had co-operated gladly out of principle or self-interest, and those who had co-existed grudgingly out of necessity. Nevertheless, the state governor proceeded against all as though they had been overt traitors. This policy was challenged by Chief Justice Aedanus Burke (1743–1802), who had served in the revolutionary militia as well as the state legislature, and would later be a strong anti-federalist and member of the first United States Congress. Burke penned a plea for discretion over the past and harmony for the future,

and in arguing that a veil of oblivion be drawn over recent
events he presented a case with obvious application far beyond
the boundaries of his own state.

NATHANIEL   WHITAKER
The Reward of Toryism
Newburyport, John Mycall, 1783
1811 Salem edition, pp. 31–51

JUDGES V, 23

Curse ye Meroz, said the Angel of the Lord, curse ye bitterly
the inhabitants thereof, because they came not to the help of
the Lord, to the help of the Lord, against the mighty. . . .

About six years ago I delivered to you a Discourse from
these words. — At that time our public affairs called on us
for the most vigorous exertions in defence of our lives, liberties, families and fortunes, which were then in great danger, not
only from the power of Britain, but more from the machinations and plots of inbred enemies. . . .

*   *   *

Our Independency is gained, but our danger is not over, nor
is our work done. Great Britain is not yet our friend, and
many of the inhabitants of Meroz are still in our land, and
many who fled from us in our distress, and would afford us
no help, yea assisted and comforted our enemies, are, under
the patronage of Britain, seeking to return, and enjoy those
privileges they used their utmost endeavours to deprive us of.
The time, the proper time is now come to execute on them
the command of God in my text, viz, *curse ye Meroz, said
the Angel of the Lord.*

If the cases are similar, the command is binding. If it can
be shown that they are not, all must own it will not apply in

the present case. But if those who had refused to come to our help against the mighty, but especially those who have gone over to, counselled, comforted and assisted the enemy, and murdered their brethren, and, with more than savage barbarity, triumphed in their torture and blood, whom the fortune of war had put into their hands: if such, I say, are not guilty of the sin of Meroz, if they can be considered as *coming to the help of the Lord against the mighty*, then indeed we ought to bless, and not curse them.

But does there need a moment's consideration to determine this point? Let the advocates for the tories of these states shew, if they can, from scripture or reason, that they have not been guilty of the sin of *Meroz*, and they will clear them of the curse. But if they stand charged, convicted and condemned for the same sin, then we are bound by invincible obligations from heaven, reason, religion, our own safety, from our forefathers and from posterity, to *curse them;* or as it is emphatically expressed in the Hebrew, *in cursing, to curse them. . . .*

*   *   *

The point I now mean to discuss, and which naturally results from the words, is this — That when God hath spirited a people, under oppression, to shake off the galling yoke of tyranny, and given them victory over their oppressors, it is His will and positive command, that *in cursing they curse* such of the community as have not joined with them in their struggle for liberty, and especially those who have aided and assisted their oppressors.

I say, such of the community, for these are not only more aggravatedly guilty than the common enemy, but they are now supposed to be in the hands of the states, and, as it is their duty, so it is in their power to curse them.

To illustrate this I shall

I. Observe as a known and undoubted truth, that the people of these States have, for years, been struggling hard for their liberties, against the mighty power of Britain. The evidence of this is so clear that it needs only to be mentioned.

II. That the tories of these States, whether still residing among us, or gone over to the enemy, are guilty of the sin of Meroz. This is evident from what I have already said, and needs no further illustration.

III. Prove the assertion in the proposition, that it is the command of God that *in cursing we curse them.*

IV. Shew what is implied in this curse.

V. Offer some thoughts as to the mode of treating them.

VI. Point out some of the fatal consequences which must attend not inflicting the curse on them.

The principal objection against this is drawn from the excellency of a tender, forgiving spirit, which is also enjoined by our Lord in his command to forgive our enemies. It must be acknowledged, that if the above assertion is repugnant to this, it ought by no means to be admitted. But those must be very ignorant of the nature of a forgiving spirit, and of Christ's command too, who suppose that executing public justice on felons and murderers, is consistent therewith. Should this be admitted, we must resign all the good and happiness of a society into the hands of thieves, robbers and assassins. Love, forgiveness of enemies and compassion, are most amiable virtues; but they degenerate into criminal weakness, as they spring from a vitiated heart, when they are employed to discharge criminals from condign punishment. Several reasons shew the weakness of this objection, and confirm the assertion.

1. The good and safety of the public require this. Calaphas the High Priest spake the truth when he said, *it was necessary that one man should die and that the whole nation should not perish.* The maxim was true; but there the application was wrong. . . . God and reason teach, that they who endanger the safety of the community, should be removed from it; for the

happiness of many is of more value than of a few: therefore we are bound to seek the good of the State, in preference to that of individuals.

But it is manifest that the State cannot be safe while the tories remain among us, unless their principles are changed, and their whole man renewed, which we have not the least reason to hope for, as no new arguments have been offered, and no new principles can be supposed to have taken place in them. For the sake of carrying the bag, they, like Judas, wish to return among us, and like him, they will sell us for thirty pieces of silver. Therefore, if we do not curse them, we shall curse the public, which will suffer more than all those traitors will ever compensate. . . .

* * *

I pass . . . to offer some thoughts as to the method of treating the inhabitants of Meroz, who have belonged, or do yet belong to these States.

Doubtless some difference should be made among those who came not to our aid against the enemy. There are different characters among them, which call for a different treatment. I shall waive a particular description of them, and rank the whole under two heads, viz. those who have been commonly called *Neuters;* and those who have taken an active part against us.

I. Neuters, if there can be any in a case of such importance. But strict neutrality I conceive, cannot be admitted, except in things in their own nature indifferent, i.e. where the interest of beings capable of happiness is not concerned. The law of love binds all men to take the side of truth, justice, liberty and happiness, and those who are not for, must be against them; . . .

Therefore when I speak of *Neuters,* I would be understood to mean those who, having knowledge of our cause, and opportunity to assist, yet have stood by as idle spectators, and have kept one foot, as it were, on American liberty, and the other on British despotism, ever ready to step into that scale where they thought their interests would be most secure.

Among these may be ranked those who, in the beginning of our troubles, talked and acted in favor of British tyranny: many such, when the current grew strong against them, shifted sides, and put on the guise of friends. We cannot determine that none of these were true penitents; but in general they have given no very convincing proofs of it. If they are, such ought to be forgiven; but we should be careful how we trust them in our public affairs.

Others, from open toryism have appeared warm for our cause, whose conversion, there is too much reason to suspect, was owing to a view of profit by speculating in trade, privateering, or of some post in the army or State; into which, men of such principles, will stick at nothing to worm themselves; and such have generally been a kind of dead weight on all our movements.

All such, of whatever description, who have not, as they had opportunity, exerted themselves in our glorious cause, if they should be allowed to continue among us, (which may perhaps be best with respect to some) yet they ought forever to be secluded from our councils, and the more manifest of them be deprived of the liberties of freemen, rendered incapable of voting for, or holding the meanest office in the States.

There is another sort who may be termed Neuters by some, who have done more mischief to the interests of freedom, and caused the shedding of more blood than any who have gone over and joined with the enemy; I mean those who have carried on a trade with the enemy during the war. These by draining off our money and sending it to the enemy, have enabled them to prosecute the war.

There may be some who have engaged in this trade inadvertently, not seeing the fatal consequences. But many have prosecuted it with determinate resolution, in defiance of conscience and all the laws that have been made against it. The first ought to be forgiven; the last should be considered as most dangerous members of the community, secluded from all the privileges of freemen, and never allowed to import goods into any of the States from any part of the world. If even those who have inadvertently dipt into this trade, cannot avoid the shocking reflection they have been instrumental in shedding the blood of their brethren; what remorse and anguish must seize those (when conscience is awake) who have knowingly assisted the enemy to murder them! But alas, the love of gold has rendered these wretched speculators and sharpers callous to all feelings of conscience, and fitted them for any line of conduct however base and unworthy! And that which adds to the distressing idea is, for those persons who have been most active in shedding so much innocent blood, will probably (as wealth begets power) in a short time become possessed of the reins of government, direct, or rather pervert the councils of the United States, lull us back into the hands of our enemies, and rivet on us the galling yoke of tyranny more firmly than ever; while the friend to his country, who has virtuously espoused her cause, and sacrificed his all in her defence, may see himself sink into silent contempt, his lands and possessions held and enjoyed by the Neuters, or by those very American British factors who, by their trade with her, have supported their plundering armies: yea even by those who have openly joined our enemies.

II. The other class of tories are, those who have taken an active part against us, of which class are all those who have deserted us and gone over to the enemy. It may be said, that even among these there are different characters, and some whose crimes are more aggravated than others. This is readily admitted, and therefore, were they in our power, they ought to receive different degrees of punishment. But the most innocent of these are highly criminal. These may be divided into two sorts; those who went to the British from fear of the issue and have remained quiet among them; and those who, from hope of favor, pensions, promotions, or interests of any kind, went over, counselled, assisted, and comforted the enemy, and lent all their aid in the war against us. These last, I should suppose, not even a semi-tory in the States could wish to return, lest those hands so long soaked in the blood of their brethren; those hearts so long inured to barbarity and slaughter, to burning and devastation, should, as it were by habitual impulse act over the same scenes with them. For, let the Ethiopian change his skin, and the leopard his spots, then will such abandoned wretches cease to do evil, and learn to do well; then, and not till then, may we hope they will be safe members of society, and leave their murder and treason.

As to the first sort, what plea can be offered for them? Why they were good and honest men; they had no enmity to us, nor to the cause of freedom, they wished to have peace, liberty and safety, but they feared the issue; viz. that Great Britain would prevail, and that they might suffer: they wish no hurt to America, but only sought safety for themselves. . . .

*   *   *

No man is so void of sense as to imagine that Great Britain would ever have begun, much less prosecuted the war for so many years, and after so many defeats and disappointments, had all those who went to her help from among us, and all who were her secret friends who resided here, been firm and resolute in the cause of freedom. . . .

*   *   *

Could sagacity discover, yet time would not allow to point out all the ill consequences which may, and probably will follow from receiving the tories into these States. I shall hint a few.

1st. This will greatly endanger the internal peace of the States. Should our rulers open the door for their return . . . they will soon find a general discontent among their constituents. They will soon hear thousands . . . lamenting, if not cursing, their folly, for risking their all and losing their dearest enjoyments on earth, next to their liberty, to purchase and defend their freedom and rights, now equally shared among their betrayers and murderers, who wisely slipt out of harm's way till they had gained the prize for them.

These cries will not expire in mere noise, but, like a loaded cannon, will make impression. Actions will naturally follow such roused passions, and internal discontents, broils and commotions, to say the least, must ensue. . . . What son of freedom can see, much less take an insult, an indelicate word, or a wry look from a tory, or sit at the feast of freedom with him when he reflects on the blood of a son, a brother, a father, shed by his impious treachery? . . .

* * *

2d. The admission of the tories will be a shameful breach of the public faith.

When the state made laws to confiscate their estates for public use; they passed that property to the people, as an encouragement for them to support the war. And will they now break their faith so solemnly pledged, and rob their constituents of their property without their consent? . . .

Besides, will not France, our faithful ally, have just cause to complain, that we have taken into our bosoms, those who while they reproached us as tools to a domestic faction of tyrants, have scandalized them as deceitful betrayers of our liberties; as having nothing in view but to enslave us, after we should be separated from Great-Britain?

3d. The restoration of the tories among us will expose us to innumerable and constant dangers which will naturally result from having in our bowels a multitude of subtil enemies, void of all honor and virtue, who, as they never will be reconciled to us, will plot our ruin, and lie ever on the watch for the most favorable advantage to avenge themselves, by betraying us into the hands and under the tyranny of Great-Britain. . . .

4th. Should we restore these murderers, we shall bring on these States the guilt of the innocent blood that has been shed in our late struggle, of which they have been the chief if not the only procurers and authors. . . . And should the honourable Congress recommend to the states to restore them, they would, as I conceive, involve themselves in the guilt of innocent blood; and should any of the general courts or assemblies of the states comply, they would partake with them in the horrid guilt; and should the people at large tamely submit, the whole land would be polluted with blood, and divine vengeance and judgments must be expected to follow. . . .

5th. Should they return they would probably soon engross the chief wealth of these states; and as wealth usually begets power, they will (as before asserted) easily possess themselves of the chief seats of government, pervert our counsels, and reduce us, by their arts, to that subjection to Great Britain which the power of her arms could not accomplish. It is too manifest that Great Britain is far from approving our independence. Necessity compelled her to a cessation of hostilities. . . . this would give her respite, to repair her strength, till a more favorable opportunity should offer to attain her wished-for end, the enslaving [of] America. If she gains this, with more rigor than ever will she claim to power "to bind us in all cases whatsoever." Then we must expect new scenes of horror and slaughter. Then will our defenceless frontiers bleed afresh; our seacoasts be infested by their fleets; our trade ruined, our sons murdered, our wives, daughters and mothers ravished, our country plundered, and our fair edifices and towns laid in ashes. These days are not far distant. The seeds are sown, yea, the plants already flourish which threaten to produce this noxious fruit. But *who will believe our report?* who will lay to heart our danger? Alas! we are so intoxicated with the joy of peace; so bewitched with the love of gain; so enamoured with the cheapness of their goods (which is the very bait to their barbed hook, that is designed for our ruin) that there is reason to fear that no warnings will move us. . . .

6th. Another and a very fatal consequence that will probably follow the re-admission of the tories, is a very great increase of taxes on the good people of these States who have borne the burden of the war. This might be easily illustrated were the subject proper for the pulpit. — But it is time to close.

AEDANUS BURKE

Cassius, *An Address to the Freemen of the State of South-Carolina*
Philadelphia, Robert Bell, 1783
pp. 3–6, 9, 17–18, 19, 26–32

FRIENDS AND FELLOW CITIZENS,

The proceedings of the late Assembly held at Jacksonborough have already excited the attention not only of this but of other States; and some of the laws then enacted are of so serious a nature; that the memory of them will last, and their consequences operate, when the authors of the measures shall be no more. By one of those laws, upwards of two hundred men who have been citizens of this State before the reduction of Charlestown, have been stripped of all their property; innocent wives and children involved in the calamity of husbands and fathers, their widows are deprived of the right of dower, their children disinherited, and themselves banished forever from this country. And this *without process, trial, examination, or hearing;* and without allowing them the sacred right of proving their innocence on a future day. Under other acts of that assembly, a number of the inhabitants are subjected to heavy fines, some to near one third, others to one eighth and some to a tenth part of their estate, real and personal, without better proof of crime than report and suggestions. Another act excludes from the freedom of voting or being elected to a seat in the legislature, almost a majority of our citizens. The crimes of all consist in the part which they were said to have taken after the reduction of South-Carolina by the British army.

One would imagine there is no free country upon earth, in which laws bringing such ruin on so many families, and so big with political mischief, would not have been publickly discussed before this day. But whether it be owing, that the measures have succeeded in breaking the spirit of the people, by filling every man with a sense of his own danger; or that the fear of the Governor's *extraordinary power*, awes men into silence; or that they are indifferent about public affairs; not a man has yet undertaken to inquire into the justice or injustice of it, or ask his neighbour how far the Legislature could effect the ruin and disgrace of so many of his fellow citizens, consistently with the laws, constitution, and happiness of his country. . . .

* * *

I must first observe, that G[overnor] R[utledge]'s proclamation on the 27th of September, 1781, was the foundation from whence sprang some of those bitter laws, and the forfeitures and disabilities abovementioned. That proclamation went entirely on the supposition, that the citizens of the State who had taken protection on the fall of the country under British usurpation, had thereby not only forfeited their lives, fortunes, and the privileges of citizenship, but had also incurred the penalty of treason against the State. This was the doctrine allowed on all hands; not only laid down by the proclamation, but advanced in both houses, and I never heard it contradicted by the *judges* or *lawyers* who ought to have known better. The proclamation indeed was supposed to have restored all those who complied with the terms of it, to their lost liberties, by joining the army within a limited time. . . .

* * *

This State, soon after the reduction of Charlestown, may be strictly said to have been conquered. Not only the capital, but every post throughout the country was in the hands of the enemy. The Governor who represented the Sovereignty of the State, had provided for his safety by flight, and all the Continental troops in South Carolina were either killed, taken, or routed.

The enemy, thus masters of the country, resolved to reduce by military force the inhabitants to obedience. And Sir Henry Clinton accordingly in the month of June 1781, issued a proclamation,

> Commanding all persons whatever inhabitants of this province, (those who were in Charlestown and Fort Moultrie at the time of their capitulations and surrender, or were then in actual confinement excepted) who shall after the 20th of June next, neglect to return to his allegiance and to his Majesty's government, will be considered as enemies and rebels to the same, and treated accordingly.

Thus a military despotism was established throughout the settlements, and to compleat this miserable scene of woes, the army under General Gates, and a division under General Sumpter, to whom we looked up as our deliverers, were entirely defeated. The country thus abandoned to a cruel, unprincipled foe, the people had no idea but that our independence was lost irrecoverably. And indeed the advantages gained by the enemy were so rapid and decisive, it was for some time apprehended thro' the other States, and even by many members of Congress, that Carolina and Georgia must in the end revert to the domination of Great Britain.

In this situation *necessity*, whose domination triumphs over all human laws pointed out to our inhabitants, that as there were neither government, laws, nor army to protect them, they were at liberty to protect themselves, as well as they could. This is the law of Nature and of Nations: And all Statesmen, the best lawyers, and most eminent writers, agree, that when an invader overruns a country, defeats the standing forces, and subverts its government, the inhabitants of such a country are justifiable to take the conqueror's protection and obey his laws; and whether the government be a monarchy or

a republick, it makes no difference, as the reason of the thing
is the same. . . .

*   *   *

Every country of which we have any account from history,
has had its day of woe and affliction, by foreign invasion, or
civil discord, as we have had. But in every one of them as soon
as the troubles were over, and the country regained; the government returned to its antient form, and the subjects were
reinstated in the participation of their rights and privileges.
And this is not only agreeable to justice, but the freedom and
liberty of the country would be destroyed if it were otherwise.
If in a republic a few could set up pretensions to superior
political merit, over the whole aggregate body of the people,
and deprive the latter of their rights and privileges, this would
be nothing more nor less than overthrowing the constitution,
seizing on the liberties of the people, and setting up an arbitrary government of the *few*. The laws of nations as well as
the rights of nature therefore dictate, that when a country
oppressed by a foreign power regains its liberty, the citizens
should be restored to all the rights and liberties they before
enjoyed.

I shall now enter on the Confiscation Act; make a few remarks on the Amercement Law; and conclude with endeavouring to prove that an Act of Amnesty and Oblivion is the only
means for restoring order, tranquillity and happiness to our
common country.

The principal difficulty I meet with on a subject where so
much may be said, is to confine myself within the narrow compass I proposed.

It is impossible not to feel distress when we reflect on the
miseries that each party in a civil war, inflict on the other as
they become uppermost. The cruel oppressions of the British,
particularly the personal insults and outrage we suffered from

their officers, after the fall of the country, is enough to make a man shudder.

Their treatment was so extravagantly outrageous, that no descriptions will even give a just idea of it; and to myself who was a witness and a sufferer, it appears like a dream, and almost incredible to me. Their cruelty to the garrison; their violation of the capitulation; their sequestration and plunder; their banishing the tender sex, our wives, and children, to a distant country, merely to gratify malice, as a day's journey would have set them down amidst their friends in their own country: During all this scene of violence and revenge, we ourselves never ceased to make the most tragical complaints, and calling heaven and earth to witness and avenge the injustice of our enemies; and yet no sooner did Providence turn things in our favour, and restore to us our country, then instead of thinking how to settle the peace and happiness of it, we took the quite contrary way, and looked about for means of doing vengeance in our turn, by way of retaliation. No sooner did we cease to fear and suffer, than our next endeavour was to make others fear and feel misery, as if it were necessary either to be suffering ruin or doing mischief. In thinking on these bitter calamities which men are so ingenious in contriving for each other, he must be more or less than man who cannot feel compassion and sorrow for the unhappy lot of human nature. . . .

*   *   *

Our act of assembly which banishes so many citizens, after reducing their families to beggary, *without hearing*, is perhaps the most furious proscription of which we have any account in all history. Sylla, the Dictator, by virtue of his *extraordinary powers*, to be revenged on the party in opposition, and enrich his own adherents, banished more citizens though he took not perhaps half the property we did. He disdained however to do it under pretence or colour of law and constitution; he did it as Lord Cornwallis sequestered our estates, and then banished

our families, by dint of military force, at the head of an army
devoted to him. . . .

*   *   *

The injustice of this measure is so enormous, that the endeavouring to prove it, is like proving that the sun now shines
at noon-day. Hearing the accused, and giving him a chance to
defend himself, is the first and most sacred rule of justice. All
sorts of laws, civil and military, laws of parliament, courts-
martial, and others, hear proof and defence; and any tribunal
that refuses to hear proof, refuses to do justice; and must
thereby suffer a ruin of character and bear an eternal stigma
and reproach on the face of its proceedings. . . .

*   *   *

The reader may judge by the preamble, whether the Committee who framed the Amercement Law paid more attention
to law and fact than they did civil language.

> Whereas many persons, inhabitants of, and owing allegiance
> to this State (some bearing high and important commissions)
> have withdrawn themselves from the defence thereof, accepted
> protection, &c.

I have proved already that our government was dissolved;
it did not exist, and of course those who are amerced could
not withdraw from its defence; As the Republic could not give
the citizen protection, which is the equivalent he receives for
allegiance, he owed none, and yet the preamble insists, "they
owed allegiance". We also see that "accepting protection" is
stated as a high crime, though I have proved above it was not.
It goes on:

> And are either within the lines of the enemy, or have omitted
> to enroll themselves and perform the duties of their country,
> pointed out and required by the Proclamation of his Excellency
> the Governor, on the 27th of September, in utter contempt of
> the executive authority, and evil example of society.

My remarks on the circumstances of the inhabitants who
were within *enemy's guards*, have, I hope, satisfied the reader

that the proclamation was improper and oppressive; that those citizens could not possibly comply with it; and that remaining where they were was perfectly justifiable.

And whereas there are others, who forgetting the social ties of kindred and humanity, and regardless of the duty and allegiance they had most solemnly sworn to their country, did actually subscribe, and pay by themselves or agents, considerable sums of money towards mounting and equipping a troop or troops of cavalry, or other military force for the service of his Britannic Majesty.

It is a maxim of our law that the greater the crime of which any citizen is accused, the clearer should be the proof to convict him of it: Yet the preamble states those facts without any sort of proof that can be called *legal*, and in utter contempt of all law — knowledge declares the facts to be a crime, that if true, were not punishable by our laws.

In all countries overrun by an invading and victorious army, nothing more common than to raise what is called *Contribution*, for the support of it; and in cities and civilized places, to make the matter easy to the people, or from an affectation of politeness, which soldiers of fortune can sometimes put on, with the bayonet at your breast, the thing is generally done by subscription. . . . Those in Charlestown who subscribed for the British cavalry, were some of them voluntiers for raising a force against us; but I believe this was not the case with all of them; the citizens were under the yoke of a tyrant, who had a thousand ways of doing him mischief.

He had favours to ask of British commanders; the restoration of indigo, rice, cattle, or other property, was a great one that day; and to be purchased only by mortifying concessions. To such people the *subscribing to British cavalry*, was another name for *contribution*. It was done perhaps under the highest necessity and compulsion. To make that a crime therefore, by a *retrospective law*, which was none before, and condemn them to near a third of their property was what I mentioned above to be punishing by an *ex post facto law*, and is arbitrary and unconstitutional. . . . The mode in which it is enforced, adds to the hardships of it. Three freeholders are chosen by the commissioners, to appraise these estates, without the controul or challenge of the owners; and however enormous the valuation they set, yet he must abide by it without appeal or redress.

The experience of all countries has shewn, that where a community splits into a faction, and has recourse to arms, and one finally gets the better, a law to bury in *oblivion* past transactions is absolutely necessary to restore tranquillity. For if after a civil war, and one party vanquished, persecution was to go on; if the fury of laws and the fierce rage of passions prevailed, while the minds of men were yet fired by deadly revenge against their fallen adversaries; this would be worse than keeping up the war: It would be carrying on hostility under the shape of justice, which is the most oppressive, and of all other injustice, excites the greatest detestation, in the most violent factions and division. . . .

*   *   *

All historians and political writers condemn the mischievous policy of pursuing the citizens with prosecutions after civil wars. Machiavel himself, tho' for violent measures on other occasions, yet strongly recommends an act of oblivion after a revolution.

Whether the necessity of a general amnesty ever occurred to the reader or not, the above observations will strike him very forcibly, as they apply so well to our present situation. However, to make this matter still clearer, I shall draw a comparison between the conduct of the British nation, on the restoration, after the grand rebellion, and of our legislature on the re-establishment of our republic in 1782.

The situation of the two countries was similar in this, that England suffered a usurpation under Cromwell, and other tyrants, and South-Carolina under the tyranny of Great-Britain: And the inhabitants of both countries, with few exceptions, submitted to the usurpers. But in other circumstances

England differed from us: British tyranny prevailed in this country only about 16 months. Their officers plundered our side boards of *plate* and wardrobes of their *contents*, to a considerable amount; and stole, or were the death of about twenty thousand negroes. In battle and cold blood they destroyed perhaps 3000 of our citizens; and they tortured our every manlike feeling, by distressing our families and insults to ourselves, whenever we fell into their hands. This is rating our damage pretty fairly. . . . these injuries vanish into nothing with what the English nation suffered in the grand rebellion. . . . It is a maxim in politics, that if a breach be made in the constitution of a government, and it be not healed, it will prove as fatal to its freedom, as a wound that is neglected and suffered to mortify, would be to the life of a man. I proved clearly that ours received a mortal one; and should the present assembly leave it *to inflame* without applying a cure, we cease to be a free people. The remedy I speak of is lenient, all healing. *Repeal at once the late election act, the amercement law, and the confiscation act, as far as it affects those who were our citizens.* — And in order that such proceedings may not be drawn into precedent hereafter, let there be a clause, *to obliterate those three acts* from the journals of both houses. *Pass an act of amnesty and oblivion, with as few exceptions as possible;* allowing such as may be excluded, a day to come in and be heard, either before the court of sessions, on a fair and public trial; or should they be men whose inveteracy, power or influence may be dangerous to the State, and are not liable to punishment by our laws; let them have a hearing before the legislature on articles of impeachment. — Provided that we mean that the word *Republic* should signify something more than mere *sound, pass an Act for dissolving the present Assembly*.

If every citizen cannot enjoy the rights of *election and representation* according to the constitution, I hope no body will be so idle as to talk of *Liberty. This, and the reversal of the three acts above mentioned*, is the measure, *and the only one* that can reconcile us to the friendship of each other; it will put an end to silly distinctions and faction: leave us at liberty to shake hands as brethren, whose fate it is to live together; and it will stand as a more lasting monument of our national wisdom, justice and magnanimity, than statues of brass or marble.

CHAPTER 8

Trust and Mistrust

The Treaty of Paris, 1783, devoted two clauses to the future treatment of the loyalists by the triumphant Americans. The provisions were cautiously worded, for the United States as then constituted could not bind the individual states to any particular course of action on the matter. Considering the widespread hostility towards the loyalists, there was little chance of their regaining their property and rights.

New York had had the highest proportion of loyalists in America, and New York City had been a British stronghold to the very end. In the face of a rigorous state policy of discrimination, Alexander Hamilton argued that both the good faith and self-interest of America demanded fair treatment for the loyalists. "Mentor" * retorted that it was the duty of the state to protect its citizens against the continued presence of traitors in their midst. It was folly, he wrote, to jeopardise the hard-won prize of independence by leniency to the loyalists. Hamilton, in rebuttal, emphasised that a man should not be punished unless found guilty of a known crime by a recognised court; it was time, he added, that revolutionary zeal take second place to consideration for the future prosperity of the whole country.

---

* "Mentor" has been frequently identified as Isaac Ledyard, an obscure individual at best; but there is no evidence to support his claim to authorship.

Definitive Treaty of Peace and Friendship between His Britannic Majesty and the United States of America. — Signed at Paris the 3rd of September, 1783.

Clauses V and VI, in British and Foreign State Papers;
London, 1841, Vol. 1, Part 1, p. 782

. . . V. It is agreed that the Congress shall earnestly recommend it to the Legislatures of the respective States, to provide for the restitution of all estates, rights, and properties which have been confiscated, belonging to real British Subjects: and also of the estates, rights, and properties of Persons resident in Districts in the possession of His Majesty's arms, and who have not borne arms against the said United States: and that Persons of any other description shall have free liberty to go to any part or parts of any of the 13 United States, and therein to remain 12 months unmolested in their endeavours to obtain the restitution of such of their estates, rights and properties as may have been confiscated; and that Congress shall also earnestly recommend to the several States, a reconsideration and revision of all Acts or Laws regarding the premises, so as to render the said Laws or Acts perfectly consistent, not only with justice and equity, but with that spirit of conciliation which, on the return of the blessings of Peace, should universally prevail. And that Congress shall also earnestly recommend to the several States, that the estates, rights, and properties of such last-mentioned Persons shall be restored to them, they refunding to any Persons who may be now in possession the *bona fide* price (where any has been given) which such Persons may have paid on purchasing any of the said lands, rights or properties since the confiscation.

And it is agreed that all Persons who have any interest in confiscated lands, either by debts, marriage settlements, or otherwise shall meet with no lawful impediment in the prosecution of their just rights.

VI. That there shall be no future confiscations made, nor any prosecutions commenced against any Person or Persons, for or by reason of the part which he or they may have taken in the present War; and that no Person shall on that account suffer any future loss or damage either in his person, liberty, or property; and that those who may be in confinement on such charges at the time of the Ratification of the Treaty in America, shall be immediately set at liberty, and the prosecutions so commenced be discontinued.

ALEXANDER HAMILTON

A Letter from Phocion to the Considerate Citizens of New-York on the Policies of the Day.

New York, Samuel London, 1784
pp. 3, 4, 7, 12–17, 19–22

While not only every personal artifice is employed by a few heated and inconsiderate spirits, to practise upon the passions of the people, but the public papers are made the channel of the most inflammatory and pernicious doctrines, tending to the subversion of all private security and genuine liberty; it would be culpable in those who understand and value the true interests of the community to be silent spectators. It is, however, a common observation, that men, bent upon mischief, are more active in the pursuit of their object, than those who aim at doing good. Hence it is in the present moment, we see the most industrious efforts to violate, the constitution of this state, to trample upon the rights of the subject, and to chicane or infringe the most solemn obligations of treaty; while dispassionate and upright men almost totally neglect the means of counteracting these dangerous attempts. A sense of duty alone calls forth the observations which will be submitted to the good sense of the people in this paper, from one who has more inclinations than leisure to serve them; and who has had too deep a share in the common exertions in this revolution, to be

willing to see its fruits blasted by the violence of rash or unprincipled men, without at least protesting against their designs.

The persons alluded to, pretend to appeal to the spirit of
Whiggism, while they endeavour to put in motion all the furious and dark passions of the human mind. The spirit of
Whiggism, is generous, humane, beneficent and just. These
men inculcate revenge, cruelty, persecution, and perfidy. The
spirit of Whiggism cherishes legal liberty, holds the rights of
every individual sacred, condemns or punishes no man without
regular trial and conviction of some crime declared by antecedent laws, reprobates equally the punishment of the citizen
by arbitrary acts of legislature, as by the lawless combinations
of unauthorised individuals: While these men are advocates for
expelling a large number of their fellow-citizens unheard,
untried, or if they cannot effect this, are for disfranchising
them, in the face of the constitution, without the judgment of
their peers, and contrary to the law of the land. . . .

*   *   *

These men, not only overleap the barriers of the constitution
without remorse, but they advise us to become the scorn of
nations, by violating the solemn engagements of the United
States. They endeavour to mould the Treaty with Great-
Britain, into such form as pleases them, and to make it mean
any thing or nothing as suits their views. They tell us, that all
the stipulations, with respect to the Tories, are merely that
Congress will recommend, and the States may comply or not
as they please.

But let any man of sense and candour read the Treaty, and
it will speak for itself. The fifth article is indeed recom-
mendatory; but the sixth is as positive as words can make it.

There shall be no future confiscations made, nor prosecutions
commenced against any person or persons, for, or by reason of
the part which he or they may have taken in the present war,
and no person shall, on that account, suffer any future loss or
damage, either in his person, liberty, or property.

As to the restoration of confiscated property which is the subject of the fifth article, the states may restore or not as they think proper, because Congress engage only to recommend; but there is not a word about recommendation in the 6th article. . . .

*　　*　　*

The *uti possiedetis, each party to hold what it possesses,* is the point from which nations set out in framing a treaty of peace; if one side gives up a part of its acquisitions, the other side renders an equivalent in some other way. What is the equivalent given to Great-Britain for all the important concessions she has made. She has rendered the capital of this state and its large dependencies. She is to surrender our immensely valuable posts on the frontier, and to yield to us a vast tract of western territory, with one half of the Lakes, by which we shall command almost the whole furr trade; she renounces to us her claim to the navigation of the Mississippi, and admits us a share in the fisheries, even on better terms than we formerly enjoyed it. As she was in possession by right of war of all these objects, whatever may have been our original pretensions to them, they are by the laws of nations to be considered as so much given up on her part; and what do we give in return? We stipulate that there shall be no future injury to her adherents among us. How insignificant the equivalent in comparison with the acquisition! A man of sense would be ashamed to compare them: A man of honesty, not intoxicated with passion, would blush to lisp a question of the obligation to observe the stipulation on our part.

If it be said that Great-Britain has only restored to us what she had unjustly taken from us, and that therefore we are not bound to make compensation — This admits of several answers. — First, That the fact is not true, for she had ceded to us a large tract of country to which we had even no plausible claim. Secondly, That however the principle of the objection might have been proper to prevent our promising an equivalent, it comes too late after the promise has been made: Thirdly, That as to the external effects of war, the voluntary law of nations knows no distinction between the justice or injustice of the quarrel; but in the treaty of peace puts the contracting parties upon an equal footing; which is a necessary consequence of the independence of nations; for as they acknowledge no common judge, if in concluding peace both parties were not to stand upon the same ground of right, there never could be an adjustment of differences or an end of war. This is a settled principle.

Let us examine the pretext upon which it is disputed. Congress, say our political jugglers, have no right to meddle with our internal police. They would be puzzled to tell what they mean by the expression. The truth is, it has no definite meaning; for it is impossible for Congress to do a single act which will not directly or indirectly affect the internal police of every state. When in order to procure privileges of commerce to the citizens of these states in foreign countries, they stipulate a reciprocity of privileges here, does not such an admission of the subjects of foreign countries to certain rights within these states operate, immediately upon their internal police? And were this not done, would not the power of making commercial treaties vested in Congress, become a mere nullity? . . .

* * *

But let it be admitted that Congress had no right to enter into this article. — Do not equity and prudence strongly urge the several states to comply with it? We have in part enjoyed the benefit of the treaty; in consequence of which, we of this state are now in possession of our capital; and this implies an obligation in conscience, to perform what is to be performed on our part. But there is a consideration which will perhaps have more force with men, who seem to be superior to conscientious obligations; it is that the British are still in possession of our frontier posts, which they may keep in spite of us; and that they may essentially exclude us from the fisheries if they

are so disposed. Breach of treaty on our part will be a just
ground for breaking it on theirs. The treaty must stand or
fall together. The wilful breach of a single article annuls the
whole. Congress are appointed by the constitution to manage
our foreign concerns. The nations with whom they contract
are to suppose they understand their own powers and will
not exceed them. If they do it in any instance, and we think
it proper to disavow the act, it will be no apology to those
with whom they contract that they had exceeded their
authority. One side cannot be bound unless the obligation is
reciprocal.

Suppose then Great-Britain should be induced to refuse a
further compliance with the treaty, in consequence of a breach
of it on our part, what situation should we be in? Can we
renew the war to compel a compliance. We know, and all
the world knows, it is out of our power? Will those who have
heretofore assisted us take our part? Their affairs require
peace as well as ours, and they will not think themselves
bound to undertake an unjust war to regain to us rights which
we have forfeited by a childish levity and a wanton contempt
of public faith.

We should then have sacrificed important interests to the
little vindictive selfish mean passions of a few. To say nothing
of the loss of territory, of the disadvantage to the whole commerce of the union, by obstructions in the fisheries; this state
would loose an annual profit of more than £50,000 *Sterling*,
from the furr trade.

But not to insist on possible inconvenience, there is a certain
evil which attends our intemperance, a loss of character in
Europe. Our Ministers write that our conduct, hitherto, in this
respect, has done us infinite injury, and has exhibited us in the
light of a people, destitute of government, on whose engagements of course no dependence can be placed.

The men who are at the head of the party which contends
for disqualification and expulsion, endeavoured to inlist a
number of people on their side by holding out motives of

private advantage to them. To the trader they say, you will
be overborne by the large capitals of the Tory merchants; to
the Mechanic, your business will be less profitable, your wages
less considerable by the interference of Tory workmen. A
man, the least acquainted with trade, will indeed laugh at such
suggestions. He will know, that every merchant or trader has
an interest in the aggregate mass of capital or stock in trade;
that what he himself wants in capital, he must make up in
credit; that unless there are others who possess large capitals,
this credit cannot be had, and that in the diminution of the
general capital of the State, commerce will decline, and his
own prospects of profit will diminish. . . .

*　　*　　*

But say some, to suffer these wealthy disaffected men to remain among us, will be dangerous to our liberties; enemies to
our government, they will be always endeavouring to under-
mine it and bring us back to the subjection of Great-Britain.
The safest reliance of every government is on mens interests.
This is a principle of human nature, on which all political
speculation to be just, must be founded. Make it the interest
of those citizens, who, during the revolution, were opposed to
us to be friends to the new government, by affording them
not only protection, but a participation in its privileges, and
they will undoubtedly become its friends. The apprehension
of returning under the dominion of Great-Britain is chimerical; if there is any way to bring it about, the measures of those
men, against whose conduct these remarks are aimed, lead
directly to it. A disorderly or a violent government may disgust the best citizens, and make the body of the people tired of
their Independence.

The embarrassed and exhausted state of Great-Britain, and
the political system of Europe, render it impossible for her
ever to re-acquire the dominion of this country. — Her former
partizans must be convinced of this, and abandon her cause as
desperate. They will never be mad enough to risk their

fortunes a second time in the hopeless attempt of restoring her authority; nor will they have any inclination to do it, if they are allowed to be happy under the government of the society in which they live. To make it practicable, if they should be so disposed, they must not only get the government of this state, but of the United States into their hands. To suppose this possible, is to suppose that a majority of the numbers, property and abilities of the United States has been and is in opposition to the revolution. Its success is a clear proof that this has not been the case; and every man of information among us, knows the contrary. — The supposition itself would show the absurdity, of expelling a small number from the city, which would constitute so insignificant a proportion of the whole, as without diminishing their influence, would only increase their disposition to do mischief. The policy in this case would be evident, of appealing to their interests rather than to their fears.

Nothing can be more ridiculous than the idea of expelling a few from this city and neighbourhood, while there are numbers in different parts of this and other states, who must necessarily partake in our governments, and who can never expect to be the objects of animadversion or exclusion. It is confirming *many* in their enmity and prejudices against the state, to indulge our enmity and prejudices against a few.

The idea of suffering the Tories to live among us under disqualifications, is equally mischievous and absurd. It is necessitating a large body of citizens in the state to continue enemies to the government, ready, at all times, in a moment of commotion, to throw their weight into that scale which meditates a change whether favourable or unfavourable to public liberty.

Viewing the subject in every possible light, there is not a single interest of the community but dictates moderation rather than violence. That honesty is still the best policy; that justice and moderation are the surest supports of every government, are maxims, which however they may be called trite, at all times true, though too seldom regarded, but rarely neglected with impunity. Were the people of America, with one voice, to ask, What shall we do to perpetuate our liberties and secure our happiness? The answer would be, "govern well" and you have nothing to fear either from internal disaffection or external hostility. Abuse not the power you possess, and you need never apprehend its diminution or loss. But if you make a wanton use of it, if you furnish another example, that despotism may debase the government of the many as well as the few, you like all others that have acted the same part, will experience that licentiousness is the forerunner to slavery. . . .

* * *

These sentiments are delivered to you in the frankness of conscious integrity, by one who *feels* that solicitude for the good of the community which the zealots, whose opinions he encounters profess, by one who pursues not as they do, the honour or emoluments of his country, by one who, though he has had, in the course of the Revolution, a very *confidential* share in the public councils, civil and military, and has as often, at least, met danger in the common cause as any of those who now assume to be the guardians of the public liberty, asks no other reward of his countrymen, than to be heard without prejudice for their own interest.

Mentor's Reply to Phocion's Letter with some Observations on Trade.
                    New York, Shepherd Kollock, 1784, pp. 5–14, 17–18

When the letter to Phocion first made its appearance, the doctrines contained in it stood so opposed to common understanding, that I was very far from supposing that any consequences arising from them, would make a reply to the letter in the smallest degree necessary; so far from it, I judged a reply would carry with it the appearance of wantonly seizing an occasion to introduce the author on the stage of politics; but experience has taught me, that passion, pomp, and plausibility, may pass even upon an enlightened people, for argument and truth.

This author, while he declaims against "heated spirits" and "inflammatory" publications, gives us a striking proof that he has, in an eminent degree, that great disqualification for a statesman, an uncontroulable warmth of temper. . . .

*   *   *

But my business is with the political part of Phocion's letter, not that which paints the author; and I would apologize for saying this much, if I was not so strong courted to it by his illiberality. For in writing and acting, I would wish however to separate the statesman or politician, and the man. . . .

*   *   *

First, then to his construction of the treaty, (which as his pamphlets are in the hands of most of the people, I will not trouble them with a long extract of it here). I beg leave to oppose to it the construction in one of the publications, under the signature of Gustavus, and leave the public to judge which is fairest.

"In the 6th article of the treaty it is provided, that no one shall suffer in his person, liberty, or property, on account of the part he might have taken in the war. The 5th article describes the persons provided for and distinguishes them into three classes: First those that are real British subjects. The second, those that were within their lines, and had not taken arms against the country. The third class are described by the provision that it made for them viz. they shall have liberty to go into any part of the United States, for twelve months, to solicit a restoration of their estates that may have been confiscated. This class must be those, who, belonging to America, have taken arms gainst their country. The first and second class, it is agreed, that Congress shall *recommend* to the states, a restoration of their property. The third it seems were too infamous for the English minister to ask any consideration for, except the wretched privilege of asking it for themselves. But I can find no where, even a request, and that only implied, that any of the three classes may dwell among us, and enjoy the immunities and privileges of citizens; for the first class are considered as former subjects, the second and third as acquired subjects of England".

But Phocion starts another difficulty: He says, to imagine, that by espousing the cause of Great-Britain, they become aliens, is to admit, that subjects may, at pleasure, renounce their allegiance to the state of which they were members, and devote themselves to foreign jurisdiction; "a principle," he adds, "contrary to law, and subversive of government".

To this I reply, that if there were nothing more in the case than their adhering to the then enemies of our country, I would readily join Phocion in opinion, that this action simply, should not be construed to amount to alienation; but it should be construed to amount to treason. So, instead of aliens, I would render them traitors, and as such, put the penal laws in force against them.

But it is by treaty, that they become aliens or subjects of England. By the treaty England adopted them as subjects, and by ratifying that treaty, the states, and this state, from the share she had in it, consented to that adoption. And this is the great benefit of the treaty to them, which Phocion says, we would violate; whereas it appears that we, who he dubs heated and designing men, are the real supporters of it.

Granting them to be aliens, Phocion continues, they cannot hold real property under our government, their real estates must then be considered as belonging to the public, this is confiscation, and thereby the Treaty is violated. I answer, that they are aliens, but aliens stipulated for. If in doing this, our ministers have exceeded the powers given them, and Congress also, by acceding to what they have done; or, if they have agreed to an article of treaty, which wars with the nature of governments, or with a particular genius of ours, let it be so declared, and also the consequence of the blunder; then we may take up the subject in another point of view. But till then we must consider it as it is, and take it for granted it is right.

But for my own part, I cannot see the inconsistency of it. Suppose the British East-India company had claims to certain lands in America, before her separation from England, and by an article of the treaty it should be agreed, that they should have the privilege of selling it, some might doubt the justice of it, but I think none can doubt the right.

To make it appear, that in removing a number of these people, prosecutions of some kind or another would be necessary, and which are forbidden by the treaty, seems to be a chief design of Phocion. Besides others which have been observed, he starts this: how will it be determined, but by prosecution, who have so adhered to the enemy, as in a legal sense to amount to crime? I answer, in the first place, that no question of law arises on this subject.

It is by treaty, and not by law, that we are to judge of them; for the ratification of that has, in effect, repealed all the laws that stood in force against them. If the treaty have not this power, then have we played the cheat, not only with England, but with every power that was represented in that Congress, which settled the terms of peace. In the second place, that the treaty itself makes a distinction that otherwise would be wanting, and all that it is necessary for the legislature in this particular is, by an act of grace to make a distinction of a very different kind; to distinguish and restore to citizenship, the deserving of those who are by treaty made subjects of England.

I presume it must by this time clearly appear, that the people we are speaking of are the subjects of England. It then remains to see, what necessity demands, and what justice and

honour will allow to be done with them; and in this investigation, let us throw aside every passion, but that which is concerned for the safety and true interest of the state.

Before I proceed, permit me to lay it down as a maxim,
that it is a principle coincident with the very nature of society,
that there be a power vested in it, in some form or other,
adequate to the purpose, not only of correcting any present
evil in it, but to prevent a probable future one.

Though I abhour all reasonings which tend to make less
heinous the dreadful sin of taking arms against our country,
both as regards the eternal law of justice, and also good policy;
yet as the country has agreed by solemn compact not to take
vengeance on those of this character in America, both our
honour and interest are concerned to preserve this compact
inviolate, so upon this occasion I shall dismiss all that passion arising from a lively recollection of what this country
sustained from them, would dictate, and speak of them
only as they respect our political safety, as a morbid humour
in our political body, which requires healthy remedies to
expel.

After a farmer has prepared his ground, would he mix cockle
with his seed wheat to grow up with and contaminate the
wholesome grain? In establishing a young empire, should we
leave the principle of sedition in its foundation? But Phocion
would tell us that this is a bug-bear danger. *Make it their
interest and they will be good subjects.* God forbid, the government should make it their interest to be its friends; for to do
this, would be to bring the principles of the government to suit
them, not them to suit *it*. The tory principle, where it has
long been entertained, and where it has long beat union with
the passions, is more fixed and immoveable than the best established government. I speak of those who have been much
concerned in government speculation. Of political opinions,
those which respect monarchical and republican governments,
are most opposed, of course most irreconcileable; they beget a

contempt for each other, in the members of the two governments.

To show that our fears for the well-being of our government
on this occasion, are founded in reason, and not ideal, beside
what has been already said, let us consider the number and
quality of the people, who, I am ashamed to say, are the
subjects of dispute, and the difference between the government
which their principles contend for, and ours.

In a monarchical government, I grant the doctrine of Phocion may obtain. There fear might make it their interest to
be good subjects; the fear of offending against the government.
But, in a republican government, the people are their own
governors. A republican government must take its shape from
the opinions of the people, and is variable, as the opinions of
its component parts may vary; hence the necessity of correcting that evil, which may spring from a corruption of
opinion, and though it may be confined to a few at first, it
may communicate to the overturning of the government. The
number of those who are in reality mal-contents in America
are not so small as may be imagined; nor are their views and
hopes so humble as many suppose.

I have said the government has a right to anticipate probable
evils. The tory principle contains in it a mortal and irreconcileable hatred to our government. That this principle will be
communicated, is too probable, when we consider the wealth,
the art, the perseverance, and fashion of many of its present
possessors.

On the other hand, let us consider the indigence which the
ravages of a long and accursed war have created in the other
party, which must cause them assiduously to attend to their
own private concerns. For though some of them still preserve
a lively attention to the government, yet in many the effect
which I have mentioned, has been wrought; and in a little time
the last spasms of the republican spirit will be over, the meager
ghost of poverty, with all her train of evils, being constantly

before them, every other consideration will yield to the spur
of necessity. In the meanwhile the mal-contents are left with
the means, and can afford the leisure to get into administration. This, fellow citizens is the condition of affairs; — I blush
to proclaim it, to which the writing and sayings of whigs tend to
bring you! — For Phocion tells you that he has been an eminent
servant of the republic in establishing her independency. If a
revolution is effected in the manner above stated, however infamous the means, yet when the revolution is compleated, it
is a just one, because it must be supposed that a majority of
opinions are for it. Therefore I say, it is importantly the duty
of the present government to anticipate such an evil, by
removing the causes of pravity of opinion. But short of a
revolution, a perversion of the principles of our government,
which is more easily wrought, may be as wounding to the
upright republican.

    With regard to England's renewing her claim to the
country, on the supposition that ill policy abroad, and anarchy
at home should invite her to it, I am clearly of opinion that it
would not be her interest to do it; for, if she should succeed,
the extent and rapid growth of the country would prevent
its being long tributary to that distant island. . . .

                    *   *   *

    There is no other way of preventing this probable corrup-
tion of opinion, but by removing the cause which I have
asserted to be the malcontents of America. Having, as we
presume, shewn the necessity, let us now, as proposed, enquire
if honour and equity will consent to the measure.

    The treaty, which justice and honour forbid us to violate,
does not, even upon so liberal a construction, as I believe
Phocion himself would give it, debar the states from making
laws that may be salutary to the government, and advantageous to the people, though in their consequences they may
operate against the interests of the subjects of England. Sup-

pose a line could be drawn, and the deserving of those, who by treaty are made subjects of England, should be re-adopted, and invested with all the privileges of citizens; and, after this, laws should be passed, giving the citizens the exclusive benefits of trade. This law would operate no more against the subjects of England that are here, than against those who are at home, except in this, the law in one case, sends these home, and in the other case, keeps them there, or rather prevents their coming here as traders. . . .

*   *   *

If the tory principle shall be repressed in this way, it is a remedy used for the health and preservation of the body politic, and as such no one, not even the tories can complain of it as unjust, though they may deprecate the hardship of the measure as applied to themselves.

In the first case, that is against laws for exclusive trade, it has been objected, that by removing these people, we remove a great part of the silver and gold out of the state. With as much propriety it may be argued against the measure, that we should remove a great part of the writing paper out of the state.

Money is a conveniency, not an article of trade; being such, wherever trade centers money will. . . .

*   *   *

Phocion's letter being essentially, though not minutely answered, . . . I will take leave of my reader. . . . From the ignorant our government is of no danger: It is the bell-wethers of the flock that we should guard against.

There is no form of government so delicate in its nature and which requires so much attention to preserve, as that which exists in the minds of these people. While corruption is kept out of it, there is no form of government so honourable to men, and so happy to the partaker of it; and when corrupted, there is no government so much to be detested and avoided. Considering things in this point of view, and considering what it has cost us to establish this government, what it would have cost us if we had failed in it, I am not willing to trifle with the acquisition. To risque it from a false notion of generosity, or because it is easy for Phocion and others to bestow the epithet of vindictive on the salutary measures that may be proposed for its preservation. We did it at the commencement of the war, and have in the whole course of it, kept it in view as a debt which we owed to posterity, to bequeath to them that liberty which we received from our ancestors. Having got this in our power by a hazardous and dreadful conflict, to suffer the inestimable acquisition to perish by neglect, would be not only to betray them but ourselves.

ALEXANDER HAMILTON
A Second Letter from Phocion to the Considerate Citizens of New-York. Containing Remarks on Mentor's Reply.
New York, Samuel Loudon, 1784, pp. 4–6, 8–9

. . . To say, that the answer of Mentor is a feeble attempt, would be no derogation from his abilities; for, in fact, the cause he espouses, admits of nothing solid; and, as one of its partizans, he is only to be blamed for not knowing its weak sides better, than to have been tempted to expose it to the experiment of a defence.

BUT before I enter farther into the subject, I shall take occasion to acknowledge, with regret, the injudicious appearance of warmth in my former letter; calculated, with many minds, to raise prejudices again the truths it contains, and liable to be misrepresented into a general censure on that part of the community, whose zeal, sacrifices and sufferings must ever render them respectable to the true friends of the revolution. I shall only observe in apology (as is truly the case) that whatever severity of animadversion may have been indulged, was wholly directed against a very small number of men, who are manifestly aiming at nothing, but the acquisition of power and profit to themselves; and who, to gratify their avidity for these objects, would trample upon every thing sacred in society, and overturn the foundations of public and private security. It is difficult for a man, conscious of a pure attachment to the public weal, who sees it invaded and endangered by such men, under specious but false pretences, either to think, or to speak of their conduct, without indignation. It is equally difficult for one, who in questions that affect the community, regards *principles* only, and not *men*, to look with indifference on attempts to make the great principles of social right, justice and honour, the victims of personal animosity or party intrigue.

MORE tenderness is indeed due to the mistakes of those, who have suffered too much to reason with impartiality, whose honest prejudices, grown into habits by the impressions of an eight years' war, cannot at once accommodate themselves to that system which the public good requires, and whose situations are less favourable to distinguishing between doctrines invented to serve the turn of a revolution, and those which must give permanent prosperity to the state.

THESE observations I have thought proper to premise, in justice to my own intentions, and I shall now proceed, as concisely as possible, to examine the suggestions of Mentor, interspersing as I go along, some remarks on objections which though omitted by him, have been urged in other shapes against the principles of Phocion.

MENTOR proposes to treat the sentiments of Phocion as a political novelty, but if he is serious, it is a proof that he is not even "tolerably well informed." They are as old as any regular notions of free government among mankind, and are to be met with, not only in every speculative Writer, on these subjects, but are interwoven in the theory and practice of that code, which constitutes the law of the land. They speak the common language of this country at the beginning of the revolution, and are essential to its future happiness and respectability.

The principles of all the arguments I have used or shall use, lie within the compass of a few simple propositions, which, to be assented to, need only to be stated.

FIRST, THAT no man can forfeit or be justly deprived without his consent, of any right, to which as a member of the community he is entitled, but for some crime incurring the forfeiture.

SECONDLY, THAT no man ought to be condemned unheard, or punished for supposed offences, without having an opportunity of making his defence.

THIRDLY, THAT a crime is *an act* committed or omitted, in violation of a public law, either forbidding or commanding it.

FOURTHLY, THAT a prosecution is in its most precise signification, an *inquiry* or *mode of ascertaining*, whether a particular person has committed, or omitted such *act*.

FIFTHLY, THAT *duties* and *rights* as applied to subjects are reciprocal; or in other words, that a man cannot be a *citizen* for the purpose of punishment, and not a *citizen* for the purpose of privilege. . . .

* * *

It was the policy of the revolution, to inculcate upon every citizen the obligation of renouncing his habitation, property, and every private concern for the service of his country, and many of us have scarcely yet learned to consider it as less than treason to have acted in a different manner. But it is time we should correct the exuberances of opinions, propagated through policy, and embraced from enthusiasm; and while we admit, that those who did act so disinterested and noble a part, deserve the applause and, wherever they can be bestowed with propriety the rewards of their country, we should cease to impute indiscriminate guilt to those, who, submitting to the accidents of war, remained with their habitations and property.

We should learn, that this conduct is tolerated by the general sense of mankind; and that according to that sense, whenever the state recovers the possession of such parts as were for a time subdued, the citizens return at once to all the rights, to which they were formerly entitled.

A B C D E F G H I J   5 4 3 2 1 7 0 6 9 8